THE BOOK OF WINZIP

THE
BOOK
OF WINZIP

FILE COMPRESSION
AND ARCHIVE
MANAGEMENT MADE EASY

Jerry Lee Ford, Jr.

**NO STARCH
PRESS**

San Francisco

Printed in the United States of America

1 2 3 4 5 6 7 8 9 10 – 04 03 02

Trademarked names are used throughout this book. Rather than use a trademark symbol with every occurrence of a trademarked name, we are using the names only in an editorial fashion and to the benefit of the trademark owner, with no intention of infringement of the trademark.

Publisher: William Pollock
Editorial Director: Karol Jurado
Cover and Interior Design: Octopod Studios
Composition: 1106 Design, LLC
Copyeditor: Judy Ziajka
Proofreader: Mu'afrida Bell
Indexer: Nancy Humphreys

Distributed to the book trade in the United States by Publishers Group West, 1700 Fourth Street, Berkeley, CA 94710; phone: 800-788-3123 or 510-528-1444; fax: 510-528-3444.

Distributed to the book trade in Canada by Jacqueline Gross & Associates, Inc., One Atlantic Avenue, Suite 105, Toronto, Ontario M6K 3E7 Canada; phone: 416-531-6737; fax 416-531-4259.

For information on translations or book distributors outside the United States and Canada, please contact No Starch Press, Inc. directly:

No Starch Press, Inc.
555 De Haro Street, Suite 250, San Francisco, CA 94107
phone: 415-863-9900; fax: 415-863-9950; info@nostarch.com; http://www.nostarch.com

The information in this book is distributed on an "As Is" basis, without warranty. While every precaution has been taken in the preparation of this work, neither the author nor No Starch Press, Inc. shall have any liability to any person or entity with respect to any loss or damage caused or alleged to be caused directly or indirectly by the information contained in it.

Library of Congress Cataloging-in-Publication Data

Ford, Jerry Lee.
The book of WinZip / Jerry Lee Ford, Jr.
     p. cm.
Includes index.
ISBN 1-886411-75-1
1. Data compression (Computer science) 2. WinZip. I. Title.
QA76.9.D33 F67 2001
005.7'6—dc21

                                                                          2001026595

DEDICATION

To Mary, Alexander and William

ACKNOWLEDGMENTS

This book is the result of the combined efforts of a number of individuals. I would like to thank Bill Pollock for working with me to make this book a reality and for his work as the book's development editor. I would also like to acknowledge the book's publicist, Amanda Staab, and Karol Jurado, its project editor.

Jerry Lee Ford, Jr.
Mechanicsville, VA

AUTHOR BIOGRAPHY

Jerry Lee Ford, Jr. is an author, educator and an Information Technology professional with over 13 years of experience. He holds a Masters in Business Administration from Virginia Commonwealth University and is a Microsoft Certified Systems Engineer. He has over 5 years of experience teaching college level IT courses and has authored of 6 other books. Jerry lives in Richmond, Virginia with his wife, Mary, and their sons, Alexander and William.

BRIEF CONTENTS

CONTENTS IN DETAIL

1

WINZIP BASICS

2

INSTALLING AND MANAGING WINZIP

3

THE WINZIP WIZARD

4

MANAGING YOUR ARCHIVES

5

WORKING WITH THE FILES IN YOUR ARCHIVES

6

WINZIP CLASSIC CONFIGURATION OPTIONS

7

WINZIP HELP

8

OPERATING SYSTEM INTEGRATION

9

BUILT-IN COMMAND-LINE SUPPORT

10

WINZIP INTERNET BROWSER SUPPORT ADD-ON

11

WINZIP SELF-EXTRACTOR ADD-ON

12

COMMAND-LINE SUPPORT ADD-ON

Appendix A
KEYBOARD SHORTCUTS

135

Appendix B
WINZIP COMMAND-LINE SUPPORT ADD-ON REFERENCE

Appendix C
WINZIP 8.01

D
GLOSSARY
149

Index
153

INTRODUCTION

Introducing WinZip

WinZip is a software application that allows you to store copies of one or more files in a single compressed file known as an *archive*. By allowing you to group related files together, WinZip helps you to organize and manage your Windows files. By providing compression, WinZip reduces the amount of disk space required to store your files.

If you are new to WinZip, you'll appreciate its intuitive design and flexibility. WinZip provides the WinZip Wizard for new users. The wizard walks you step by step through the most commonly performed WinZip tasks. All you'll have to do is select choices from the options that are presented to you, and the wizard takes care of the work for you.

Once you have become comfortable working with WinZip, you'll want to graduate from the WinZip Wizard to the WinZip Classic interface. From here, you will be able to perform any WinZip task. WinZip Classic provides you with total control over your archives. In addition to allowing you to create new archives, WinZip lets you work with them in many other ways. For example, you can open an archive and extract its contents, add new files to an archive, and print archive contents. You can also protect files stored in archives, with passwords.

The goal of this book is to teach you everything that you need to know to get started working with WinZip quickly, while also presenting a complete review of all WinZip features. You'll learn how WinZip works, and how you can use it to work faster and smarter.

How This Book Is Organized

This book is organized into 12 chapters and 4 appendices. The first two chapters introduce you to WinZip and help you get it installed and running.

The next three chapters show you how to use WinZip to get things done. Chapter 3 teaches you how to work with the WinZip Wizard to create, modify, and open archives. Chapters 4 and 5 provide detailed coverage of WinZip Classic: WinZip's advanced user interface. Here you learn more about what makes WinZip tick, and how to perform every major WinZip task.

The goal of the next two chapters is to help you work better with WinZip. WinZip is a highly configurable application. Chapter 6 shows you how to configure WinZip to make it work the way you want it to. As easy as WinZip is to use, there will be times when you have a question or need help getting something done. Chapter 7 introduces you to the WinZip help system and shows you how it is organized and how to use WinZip's help system to find the information you want.

Chapters 8 and 9 describe how WinZip is designed to integrate with Microsoft Windows. Chapter 8 points out the many places in Windows where WinZip has added new functionality and shows you how to use it to work smarter and faster. If you like working from the command line, then you will really appreciate WinZip's built-in command line support, which is covered in Chapter 9. You get a quick lesson on how the Windows command line works and see examples of how you can use it to work with WinZip.

The last three chapters present information on three related but optional WinZip applications that you can use to extend WinZip capabilities. Chapter 10 introduces the WinZip Internet Browser Support Add-on, which allows you to use WinZip to streamline the process of working with archives that you download from the Internet. Chapter 11 shows you how to install and work with the WinZip Self-Extractor 2.2 Add-on, which allows you to create intelligent archives. Chapter 12 explains how to use the WinZip Command-Line Support Add-on and demonstrates how it expands on WinZip's built-in command-line capabilities.

This book also provides four appendices. Appendix A provides a list of WinZip keyboard shortcuts that you can use to invoke WinZip commands right from your computer's keyboard. Appendix B provides a command reference for the WinZip Command Line Add-on application. Appendix C covers the new features provided in the beta version of WinZip 8.1. Appendix D provides a glossary of terms that you can use as a reference when reading this book and working with WinZip.

What You Will Need

All that you need to complete this book is a copy of WinZip and a computer running one of the Microsoft Windows operating systems. This book also provides coverage of several WinZip add-on components; you may also want to get a copy of each of them as well. The list of add-on modules includes the following:

- The WinZip Command-Line Support Add-on
- The WinZip Self-Extractor 2.2 Add-on
- The WinZip Internet Browser Support Add-on

You can download a trial version of WinZip and copies of each of the add-on modules from www.winzip.com.

Who Should Read This Book

This book is written for the beginning computer or Internet user who wants to know how to work with WinZip. Whether you just want to know how to "unzip" archives or want to know how to create and distribute your own archive files, this book can help. Prior experience with WinZip or other similar applications is not expected. This book will show you everything that you need to know from the ground up. As long as you have previous experience with Windows and one other application, this book will provide the rest.

Intermediate and advanced users should find the material presented in the latter chapters helpful, particularly the information in Chapter 12, which shows you how to create self-extracting archives. Whether you just want to email a few files to friends, more efficiently store large files on your computer, or distribute files from a website to millions of people around the world, *The Book of WinZip* can help.

Conventions Used in This Book

To make *The Book of WinZip* as useful and understandable as possible, a number of conventions have been used. These include the following:

Italics. New terms appear in italics when they are first introduced.

NOTEs: Throughout this book, you will find text labeled as notes; notes provide information that may be useful though not necessarily essential to the topic being covered.

TIPs: Tips provide helpful suggestions for saving time or show alternate ways to perform tasks.

1

WINZIP BASICS

WHAT YOU'LL LEARN
In this chapter, you will:

- Learn the benefits of archive management

- Review the characteristics of Zip files

- Examine WinZip and Windows integration

- Learn about the different WinZip interfaces

- Learn about other software applications that work with WinZip

If you have spent much time on the Internet, chances are good that you have encountered compressed files. These compressed files, commonly called zipped files (though *zip* is only one form of compression), are compressed, or shrunken, files or collections of files.

Compressing, or zipping, files shrinks them, making them easier to store because they require less storage space. Compressed files also save you time when you need to upload or email a file to someone; compressing a large file before emailing it can significantly reduce the amount of time required to send the email.

Compressed files provide a fast and efficient way to organize and transport data. The WinZip Windows software allows you to easily work with Zip files—creating, modifying, and extracting (decompressing) their contents. But WinZip does more than just manage Zip files. As you will see later in this chapter, WinZip works with many different types of compressed files.

WinZip does much more than simply store collections of compressed files. It allows you to view compressed files without uncompressing them, automatically install their contents, print a file listing, and even create self-extracting Zip files. A *self-extracting* Zip file is a compressed file that anyone can uncompress simply by opening it. In addition to their compressed file contents, self-extracting files contain a small hidden decompression program added by WinZip that automatically executes when the self-extracting file is opened.

WinZip is the only tool that you will need to perform any of the following tasks:

- Unzip compressed files that you download from the Internet
- Create your own compressed files to speed up your email and Internet uploads
- Add multiple files to a single Zip file
- Create Zip files that can unzip themselves

By compressing and grouping your files into archives, WinZip can save you both time and valuable disk space. WinZip makes learning to perform these tasks easy by providing you with a step-by-step wizard that walks you through each task. Later, when you are ready, WinZip provides a more advanced user interface that lets you work even more efficiently.

What Is an Archive?

A Zip file can contain one or more files. A Zip file with multiple files is called an *archive* file. When you compress files using WinZip or another compression tool, you can reduce the size of a file dramatically—sometimes by as much as 90 percent. Thus, you save storage space and time uploading or downloading these shrunken files.

Zip files are especially useful for creating email attachments (because they shrink file size) and for storing files across multiple floppy disks that otherwise would be too large for only one floppy. Compressed files are used extensively on the Internet to speed up downloads.

NOTE *The terms* Zip file *and* archive *are used synonymously throughout this book.*

TIP *If your Internet Service provider limits the size of your outgoing emails or the number of attachments you can add to your email, use WinZip to collect and compress your email attachments into a single archive.*

Types of Archives

When surfing the Internet, you are likely to find many different types of compressed files, the qualities of which will vary. Most archive formats support compression, though some will store only a single file. Table 1-1 lists the various archive file types supported by WinZip. ZIP and CAB file types are the most commonly seen; the ARC, ARJ, and LZH file formats are rarely seen any more. Other file types, such as TAR, Z, and GZ, are more common to the Unix operating system than they are to Windows, so if you use only Windows you will rarely, if ever, encounter them.

COMMONLY SEEN

Table 1-1: WinZip-Supported Archive Formats

File Extension	File Type	Supports Compression	Supports Grouping	Spans Multiple Disks	Requires External Progam	Self-Extracting
ZIP	ZIP	Yes	Yes	Yes	No	Yes
TAR	Tape Archive File	No	Yes	No	No	No
Z	Gzip File	Yes	No	No	No	No
GZ	Gzip File	Yes	No	No	No	No
CAB	Cabinet File	Yes	Yes	No	No	No
ARC	ARC File	Yes	Yes	No	Yes	No
ARJ	ARJ File	Yes	Yes	No	Yes	No
LZH	LZH File	Yes	Yes	No	Yes	No

(handwritten annotation: TAR, Z, GZ bracketed and labeled "UNIX")

As Table 1-1 shows, WinZip lets you create archives that span multiple disks, thus allowing you to create large archives and copy them to floppy disks. When an archive is too big to fit on a single disk, WinZip automatically configures the archive so that it can be stored across as many floppy disks as needed.

As Table 1-1 also shows, WinZip supports alternative archive file types that require external programs in order for WinZip to work with them, such as ARC, ARJ, and LZH archives. These external programs are applications that have been developed by parties other than WinZip Computing to manage specific compression types. More information about where to find these programs and how to install and work with them is provided in Chapter 6, "WinZip Classic Configuration Options."

NOTE *WinZip also supports UUencoded, XXencoded, BinHex, and MIME file types. These file types are used to send files via Internet email.*

Regardless of which of these file formats you need to work with, WinZip allows you to handle them using the same interface and procedures.

Zip files are by far the most popular archive format used on the Internet and have become the de facto standard for Windows users. Therefore, the chances are pretty good that you may never need to work with any other archive type. WinZip stores the archives that it creates as Zip files with a .zip file extension. However, WinZip also works with many competing file type formats, such as TAR, Gzip, and CAB files, making it the only archive management tool that you will need. Except for the archive creation process, WinZip handles all archive file types in the exact same way, so you have to learn only one way of doing things.

Demystifying Compression

While you don't need to be an expert on file compression, a basic understanding of how compression works under the covers will make it easier and more intuitive for you to use WinZip. (You can skip this section if you want to, but it won't hurt to read it.)

There are a number of ways to compress files, the most basic of which is to eliminate repeated patterns within the original files. For example, say you wanted to reduce the size of the following text excerpt from one of Winston Churchill's many World War II speeches:

We shall go on to the end, we shall fight in France, we shall fight on the seas and oceans, we shall fight with growing confidence and growing strength in the air, we shall defend our Island, whatever the cost may be, we shall fight on the beaches, we shall fight on the landing grounds, we shall fight in the fields and in the streets, we shall fight in the hills; we shall never surrender, and even if, which I do not for a moment believe, this Island or a large part of it were subjugated and starving, then our Empire beyond the seas, armed and guarded by the British Fleet, would carry on the struggle, until, in God's good time, the New World, with all its power and might, steps forth to the rescue and the liberation of the old.

This excerpt consists of 736 characters, including spaces. One way to compress this file would be to use a technique knows as a *dictionary-based approach*. When using this technique, you create a list of words or text patterns that are repeated throughout the text and define them using a short code.

For example, the following list represents a simple dictionary consisting of 48 letters and spaces that define nine patterns found in the text file. The first word or pattern is the word *shall*, which is recorded in the dictionary and assigned a value of 1. The second word or pattern added to the dictionary is the word *fight*, which is assigned a code of 2. Likewise, seven additional patterns are added to the dictionary.

1	shall	**6**	at
2	fight	**7**	en
3	the	**8**	on
4	we	**9**	with
5	an		

By substituting the newly defined code for each word or pattern, we can generate a new, compressed file, as shown here:

We 2 go 8 to 3 7d, 4 2 2 in Fr5ce, 4 2 2 8 3 seas 5d oce5s, 4 2 2 9growing c8fid7ce 5d growing str7gth in 3 air, 4 2 def7d our Isl5d, wh6ever 3 cost may be, 4 2 2 8 3 beaches, 4 2 2 8 3 l5ding grounds, 4 2 2 in 3 fields 5d in 3 streets, 4 2 2 in 3 hills; 4 2 never surr7der, 5d ev7 if, which I do not for a mom7t believe, this Isl5d or a large part of it 4re subjug6ed 5d starving, 3n our Empire bey8d 3 seas, armed 5d guarded by 3 British Fleet, would carry 8 3 struggle, until, in God's good time, 3 New World, 9all its po4r 5d might, steps forth to 3 rescue 5d 3 liber6i8 of 3 old.

This new file consists of 584 characters; add to this the size of the dictionary, and you end up with a total file size of 629 characters, representing a 15 percent reduction in size.

To reduce the size of the compressed file even further, you could add dictionary entries. As the size of a text file grows, so does the opportunity to expand the dictionary and further compress the file, which, when the dictionary approach is combined with other compression techniques, can be shrunk by up to 90 percent.

Why Use Zip Files?

Zip files are the standard archive format for Windows operating systems. Like WinZip, virtually every other archive management application supports them. This almost universal acceptance makes Zip files the obvious archive file type of choice. WinZip can create only Zip archives. However, the rest of WinZip's functions (including viewing and extraction) apply to all WinZip-supported archive types. In other words, while WinZip cannot create new CAB or TAR archives, it can still view their contents and uncompress them. Zip files let you group multiple files into a single Zip file, so if you have a collection of files to store or send, you can store them all in a single Zip file. In addition, Zip files allow you to create archives that can span multiple disks. These three features are depicted in Figure 1-1.

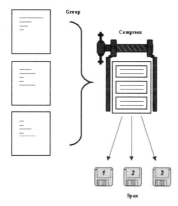

Figure 1-1: Three main benefits of using WinZip and Zip files are file grouping, compression, and disk spanning

To summarize, Zip files provide the following basic benefits:

- **Reduced storage requirements**. Zip files require less disk space than their uncompressed counterparts.

- **Reduced transmission time**. Because Zip files are smaller, they take less time to download or upload over the Internet.

- **Better organization**. Because they take up less disk space than the original files, Zip files enable efficient storage of seldom-used files.

- **Faster email**. Compressing multiple files into a single Zip file before attaching them to an email reduces the size of your email and thus makes transmission faster.

- **Reduced download time**. Websites can use Zip files to package their software products for faster download.

- **Reduced network requirements**. Because zipping files shrinks them, Zip files require fewer network resources than uncompressed ones when copied across a network.

Why Some Files Compress More Than Others

Compression is the process of reducing the amount of space required to store a file. Some text files can compress as much as 90 percent, while other types of files may compress to only about 50 percent of their original size. As you can see, not all files compress equally. In fact, some types of files cannot be compressed at all. This is because they are automatically compressed when they are first created. This is especially true for many types of graphic files. For example, two popular types of graphics files, GIF and JPEG, are automatically compressed by the applications that create them. Since these types of files are already compressed, you will not see a reduction in size when you add them to a Zip archive.

However, just because you cannot compress certain file types does not mean you cannot still benefit by adding them to Zip files. Often the convenience of grouping a collection of files into a single archive provides enough of a benefit to more than justify storing and transporting your files inside Zip files.

NOTE *Compressing a compressed file may result in an archive that is larger than the original file.*

WinZip Overview

WinZip, shown in Figure 1-2, is an incredibly easy-to-use tool for creating, modifying, and extracting the contents of Zip files. WinZip also provides several advanced capabilities, including: the ability to create Zip files that can be stored or spanned across multiple floppy disks; the ability to configure a virus scanner to scan the contents of your archives for viruses before you extract them; and even the ability to create an archive (an executable file) that you can open by simply double-clicking it.

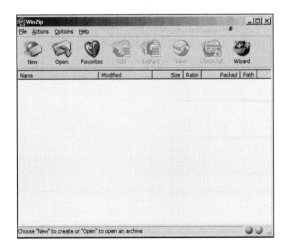

Figure 1-2: The WinZip Classic graphical user interface provides an intuitive point-and-click tool for managing all your archives

Supported Operating Systems

As of the writing of this book, the current version of WinZip is WinZip 8.*x*. It provides support for all of the following operating systems:

- Windows 95
- Windows 98
- Windows ME
- Windows NT 4
- Windows 2000
- Windows XP

NOTE *WinZip 8.x does not support Windows 3.1. If you are a Windows 3.1 user, you will need to download a copy of WinZip 6.3.*

WinZip is available in a number of different languages, including German, Japanese, and French.

WinZip Is Shareware

You will not see WinZip for sale in your local computer store (at least not at this writing). WinZip is a software program that is distributed as shareware. *Shareware* is an online distribution format that allows you to download, install, and test a copy of the program before deciding whether to purchase it. The WinZip download allows you to try the product for free for 21 days, after which time you are required to purchase it or discontinue using it. It can be downloaded from the WinZip website at www.winzip.com, as shown in Figure 1-3, or from any of a number of shareware sites, including www.download.com that as of the writing of this book has already hosted over 52,000,000 WinZip downloads.

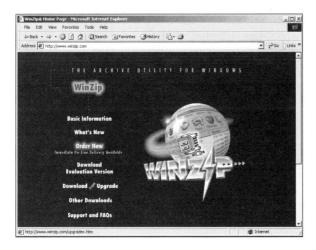

Figure 1-3: Because it is a shareware product, you may evaluate WinZip for 21 days before deciding whether to purchase it

What's New in WinZip 8.x

WinZip 8.*x* introduces a rich new set of features to WinZip. This section highlights some of these features and provides a quick tour for current WinZip users who want to know what WinZip 8.*x* has in store for them.

Zip and Email. Creates a temporary Zip file and attaches it to an email message using your default email application. (The temporary file is automatically deleted after you send the email.)

Screen and Theme Saver Installer. Allows WinZip to automatically install any screen savers or themes contained in a Zip file.

New WinZip Wizard Options. The WinZip Wizard has been expanded so that it can now create new Zip files and add files to existing Zip files.

Subfolder Support. WinZip now handles subfolders in the same way that Windows does by automatically adding their contents to Zip files when selected.

Explorer-like Toolbar. WinZip now includes a new (optional) Explorer-like toolbar.

Tool Tips. Tool tips now automatically appear when you move the pointer over an archive; they display the number of files in an archive and a comment message if one has been added to the archive.

Enhanced Comment Support. WinZip now displays an icon in its status bar representing a comment if one has been added to the Zip file.

TIP *If you are a registered user of an English version of WinZip, you are entitled to a free upgrade to WinZip 8.x. This will allow you to take full advantage of WinZip's latest features and capabilities.*

Windows Integration

WinZip provides complete integration with Windows operating systems. Not only does it look and behave like a typical Windows application, but it also adds a number of features to Windows. These features include the following:

- Opening an archive by double-clicking it
- Creating archives using drag and drop
- Adding files to archives using drag and drop
- Unzipping an archive by dragging and dropping its contents onto your desktop
- Unzipping archive files and automatically loading them into other applications, such as Microsoft Word
- Automatically opening any archive by dragging it onto an open WinZip window
- Automatically running an executable program contained in a Zip file (for example, .exe, .com, and .bat files) after unzipping it

- Viewing the contents of files without unzipping them from their archives

Upon installation, WinZip integrates itself with Windows in many other ways. In addition to adding itself to the Start menu and setting itself up so that Windows knows to start WinZip when you double-click a Zip file, WinZip adds a link to the Windows context menus that appears when you right-click a file's icon. For example, after installing WinZip you will see new file options if you right-click any regular Windows file, as shown in Figure 1-4.

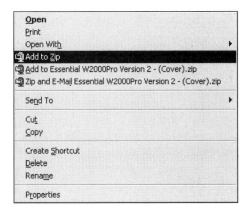

Figure 1-4: After installing WinZip, you can right-click any file and see WinZip menu options for adding the file to an archive or zipping and emailing the file

When you right-click any Zip file, you'll see a different set of WinZip context menu options. In this case, you'll see options that allow you to unzip an archive, create a self-extracting Zip file, and attach an archive to an e-mailemail, as demonstrated in Figure 1-5.

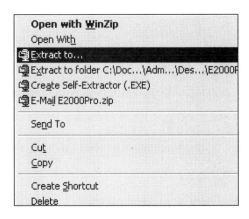

Figure 1-5: Once installed, WinZip allows you to right-click any archive and perform WinZip operations on it

WinZip User Interfaces

WinZip is known as a tool that makes working with Zip files easy. However, many people do not realize that WinZip can do more than just compress and uncompress files. For example, it provides three different ways to work with your archives, each of which is designed to accommodate a different type of user. These are the options:

- **WinZip Wizard**. This interface, designed for beginners, steps you through most WinZip tasks, including creating Zip files, adding new files to existing Zip files, and extracting the files in a Zip file.
- **WinZip Classic**. This interface, for more advanced WinZip users, provides access to all WinZip functionality, including that provided by the WinZip Wizard.
- **Command-Line Interface**. This text-based interface allows you to work with WinZip from the Windows command prompt.

Each of these options represents an increasing level of complexity and requires additional levels of skill. We will cover each completely in this book.

WinZip Components and Add-ons

Because of its ease of use, many people tend to think of WinZip as a simple tool, but WinZip can perform some pretty complex tasks. (It's just good at making what it does look easy.) As this book will demonstrate, WinZip is a powerful tool that you can use to store and transport your files more easily.

WinZip is designed to work with several other applications that can be used to enhance or extend WinZip's built-in capabilities. Figure 1-6 shows WinZip's relationship to each of these applications.

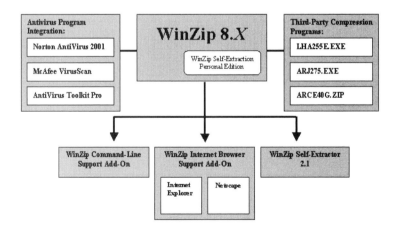

Figure 1-6: WinZip is the key component for integrating a collection of applications

WinZip's relationship to each of these applications is explained here.

Antivirus Software. If you have an antivirus program installed, you may be able to configure WinZip to use it to scan the contents of Zip files for viruses. WinZip will automatically detect certain antivirus programs such as Norton AntiVirus and McAfee VirusScan and can be configured to work with many others. (You'll learn more about how WinZip can work with antivirus programs in Chapter 5, "Working with the Files in Your Archives.")

External Compression Programs. These are third-party compression programs designed to work with specific types of compressed files. You can configure WinZip to use these programs so that it can work with more than just the .zip format. (You'll learn how in Chapter 6, "WinZip Classic Configuration Options.")

WinZip Command Line Add-on. This optional program increases the number of things you can do with WinZip when working from the Windows command prompt. (You'll learn more in Chapter 12, "Command-Line Support Add-on.")

WinZip Internet Browser Add-on. This optional program adds a number of WinZip capabilities to your Internet Explorer or Netscape Communicator web browser. (You'll learn more about the WinZip Internet Browser Add-on in Chapter 10, "WinZip Internet Browser Support Add-on.")

WinZip's Self-Extraction Personal Edition. This feature allows you to create Zip files that uncompress themselves. (You'll learn more about this in Chapter 5, "Working with the Files in Your Archives.")

WinZip Self-Extractor. This optional program lets you create advanced self-extracting Zip files with features not found in WinZip's Self-Extraction Personal Edition, such as the ability to display messages to users while the Zip file uncompresses. (You'll learn more in Chapter 11, "WinZip Self-Extractor Add-on.")

2

INSTALLING AND MANAGING WINZIP

WHAT YOU'LL LEARN
In this chapter, you will:

- Verify WinZip system requirements
- Download and install WinZip
- Upgrade an earlier version of WinZip
- Register your copy of WinZip
- Uninstall WinZip

This chapter tells you how to install, upgrade, register, and uninstall WinZip and how to obtain technical assistance from WinZip Computing.

WinZip System Requirements

WinZip 8.*x* requires Windows 95 or higher or Windows NT 4, 2000, or XP. It will not run on Windows 3.1 or earlier versions of Windows NT. To run WinZip on Windows 3.1, you'll need to install WinZip version 6.3 or lower. You can find both the current WinZip version, 8.*x*, and WinZip 6.3 at most major shareware download sites (www.download.com is a good one) or on the WinZip home page (www.winzip.com).

TIP   *If you are buying WinZip for your company and need more than ten copies, consider buying a site license. A site license allows you to download one copy of WinZip and then install it on as many computers as you purchased copies for.*

Installing WinZip

To install WinZip 8.*x*, you first need a copy of the program. The easiest way to get WinZip is to go to www.winzip.com and click on the Download Evaluation Version link. The following procedure describes how to install WinZip. If you already have a previous version of WinZip installed, you can perform an upgrade, which is described later in this chapter.

1. To install WinZip 8.*x*, double-click the WinZip8x.exe file icon, shown in Figure 2-1, to begin the installation process.

NOTE *WinZip 8 is the current version of WinZip as of the writing of this book. From time to time, as WinZip is updated or problems corrected, WinZip may be released with a newer version number. Unless major new features are added, its primary version number (8, for instance) will usually just be modified (as in 8.3 or 8.5), since its basic features remain unchanged. To keep things simple, we'll refer to this version as WinZip 8.x.*

Figure 2-1: Double-click the winzip80 icon to begin the WinZip installation process

2. Click Setup to begin, as shown in Figure 2-2. If you want to abort the installation process, click Cancel instead.

NOTE *If you click Info in the WinZip 8.0 Setup dialog box, you will see that the installation file is a self-extracting Zip file created using WinZip Self-Extractor 2.2. To learn more about WinZip Self-Extractor, see Chapter 11, "WinZip Self-Extractor Add-on."*

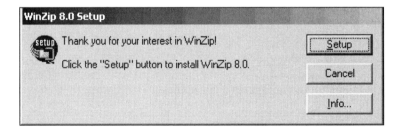

Figure 2-2: Click Setup to begin installing WinZip or Cancel to abort the installation process

3. The installer asks you where to store the WinZip files. The default location is your Program Files folder, which should be just fine. To accept this location, click OK.

4. A quick overview of WinZip's features appears. Read them, and click Next.

NOTE *Press F1 from this point forward for help.*

5. The WinZip License Agreement and Warranty Disclaimer box appears. Click View License Agreement to review the agreement's terms and click Yes if you accept them.

6. You're next asked whether to view or print the WinZip Quick Start Guide, which offers a brief overview of WinZip and its various functions. Choose an option and then click Next.

TIP *To view or print the WinZip Quick Start Guide later, open WinZip Classic and select Help • Contents • Introduction to WinZip and then the WinZip Quick Start Guide. You can also view the Quick Start Guide from the WinZip Wizard by clicking Help and then selecting the WinZip Quick Start Guide from the list of topics at the bottom of the dialog box.*

7. Select the default startup mode for WinZip as shown in Figure 2-3. You have two options: WinZip Wizard and WinZip Classic. The WinZip Wizard automates many of WinZip's processes and is recommended for new WinZip users. WinZip Classic offers more features and is the better choice for experienced WinZip users. Choose an option and then click Next.

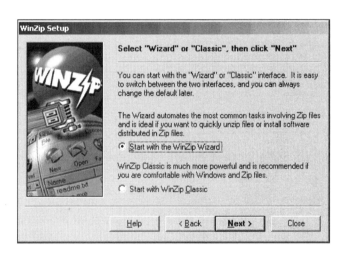

Figure 2-3: Select either WinZip Wizard or WinZip Classic, depending on your experience

TIP *You can easily switch between WinZip's Wizard and Classic versions by clicking a button in the program.*

NOTE *If you choose WinZip Classic, you are asked to choose between Express and Custom Setup. The Express option is fastest and chooses file locations for you. The Custom option lets you specify a number of configuration options, but if you're not familiar with WinZip, it will be hard to decide which configuration options are right for you. Chapter 6, "WinZip Classic Configuration Options," covers all of these configuration options in detail and explains how to change them once the installation is complete. The remaining instructions in this section assume that you have selected the WinZip Wizard installation option.*

8. The installation program searches your hard disk for folders with Zip files (Figure 2-4). Any folders that are found with Zip files are then added to the list of Favorite Zip Folders. Favorite Zip Folders is a WinZip feature that allows you to view all your Zip files as if they were actually stored in a single location. More information on Favorite Zip Folders is available in Chapter 3, "WinZip Wizard" and Chapter 4, "Managing Your Archives." You can choose to search your entire hard disk (searching every folder on your hard disk), or to do a quick search, which searches only folders likely to contain Zip files, such as AOL or CompuServe Download folders. If you have a few extra moments you might as well select the Search Entire Hard Disk option and start off with all your Zip files organized into your Favorite Zip Folders. Select an option and click Next.

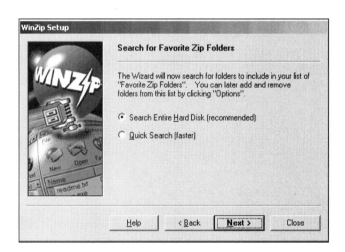

Figure 2-4: The WinZip installer can scan your hard disk for Zip files and add them to a Favorite Zip Folders collection, where you can easily manage them

9. When the search for Zip files is completed, you'll be shown the results of the search; you should see something like Figure 2-5. You'll then be asked how you want to proceed. You can choose to add folders that WinZip recognizes as download folders to the Favorite Zip Folders grouping or to add every folder in which a Zip file was found. I'd recommend selecting the option to add all folders containing Zip files. This way you'll have easy access to every Zip file on your computer. Choose an option and click OK, or choose Cancel to continue with the installation without adding any folders to the Favorite Zip Folders collection.

TIP *To search for folders containing Zip files at any time, click the Favorites icon in WinZip Classic and then click Search. If you are using WinZip Wizard you can tell WinZip to search for new Zip folders by clicking on the Search button, which is displayed when unzipping or updating a Zip file with the wizard.*

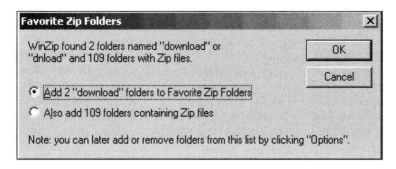

Figure 2-5: Specify whether to include your Zip files in the Favorite Zip Folders collection

10. The WinZip installer adds the specified folders to your Favorite Zip Folders list and displays a dialog box showing the results of the operation. Click Next.

11. You can now configure WinZip file *associations,* which tell Windows which compressed files WinZip should open. Click Associations to view the default list of archive file types, shown in Figure 2-6, or click Next to accept the defaults. Any time you open a file with one of the file extensions listed, Windows will automatically load it into WinZip. I recommend that you leave all selections enabled making WinZip your default application for all archive files.

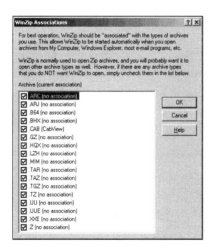

Figure 2-6: View and modify the archive file types to be automatically associated with WinZip

12. WinZip installation is complete. Click Close to finish the installation process, or click Next to begin working with WinZip.

A WinZip program group is added to your Start menu, with the items shown in Figure 2-7.

Figure 2-7: The WinZip program group on the Windows Start menu offers easy access to WinZip and related resources

The WinZip items on your Start menu include the following:

Online Manual. A copy of WinZip's user guide.

ReadMe.txt. Installation instructions and references to other useful documentation.

Uninstall WinZip. The program used to uninstall WinZip from your computer.

What's New. A brief overview of the new features found in this version of WinZip.

WinZip.8.0. The button to start WinZip.

WinZip is now ready for use. To begin using it, click Start • Programs • WinZip or click the WinZip shortcut on your desktop.

WinZip's Tip of the Day

By default, WinZip displays a Tip of the Day every time it starts, as shown in Figure 2-8, except when WinZip is started by opening a compressed file.

These tips tell you about particular WinZip features or how to perform specific tasks. To see additional tips, click Next Tip, or click Close to close the tip window. To control the way WinZip displays these tips, select from the options in the drop-down list in the lower-left corner of the screen: Always show tips at startup, Show tips at startup if not opening an archive, or Never show tips at startup.

TIP   *If you select the Never show tips at startup option and then decide that you would like to see WinZip tips again, you can restore the tip screen by opening WinZip Classic and selecting the Tip of the Day option on the Help menu.*

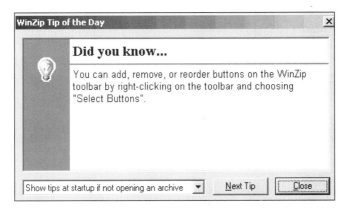

Figure 2-8: WinZip Tip of the Day

Upgrading from a Previous Version of WinZip

Registered users of an English version of WinZip may upgrade for free, and upgrading is as easy as installing for the first time. To upgrade your copy of WinZip, you need to download a new copy of the program. The easiest way to get WinZip is to go to www.winzip.com and click on the Download Evaluation Version link. The same download file used to perform an upgrade of WinZip is also used to perform a new installation. To upgrade your copy of WinZip, follow these steps:

1. Close any open programs, including WinZip.

2. Start the WinZip installation process by double-clicking the WinZip8x.exe file icon and then clicking Setup, just as if you were performing a first-time installation.

3. When asked where you want to store the WinZip files, make sure that you install them in the same place as the current WinZip source files, as shown in Figure 2-9.

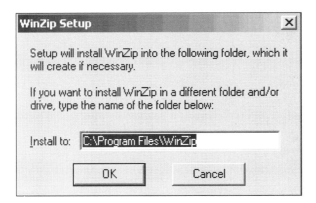

Figure 2-9: When upgrading WinZip, make sure to install the new WinZip files in the same place as the current ones

TIP *By default, WinZip is installed in your C:\Program File\WinZip folder, so unless you changed this location during the initial installation of WinZip, you should find the WinZip files here.*

4. Continue with your upgrade by following the prompts, just as you would for a first-time installation.

Registering Your Copy of WinZip

When you start an unregistered trial copy of WinZip, the dialog box shown in Figure 2-10 appears reminding you that you are using an evaluation version. Here you can choose the following:

View Evaluation License. View the terms of the WinZip Evaluation License agreement.

Enter Registration Code. Enter your WinZip registration number to make this box go away.

I Agree. To use the trial version of WinZip, you must agree to the Evaluation License agreement each time you use it.

Quit. Exit WinZip.

Ordering Info. Find out how to order a licensed copy of WinZip.

You'll have 21 days to try WinZip before you need to register it. To purchase your copy, click the Order Now link at www.winzip.com and complete the WinZip order form. If you choose electronic delivery, you will instantly receive your registration number. If you choose mail delivery, your registration number will be included with your packaged version of WinZip.

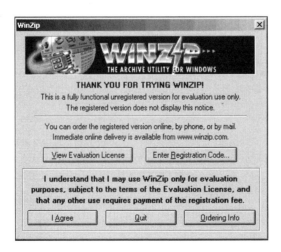

Figure 2-10: A registration reminder dialog box appears each time you start a trial, unregistered version of WinZip

Entering Your Registration Number

Once you have your registration number, register your trial copy by clicking Enter Registration Code in the initial Windows dialog box and then following the steps listed here.

You can also register your copy of WinZip from the WinZip Wizard and WinZip Classic interfaces. From the WinZip Wizard, click About and then Register. From WinZip Classic, click the About WinZip option on the Help menu and then click Register.

1. Click Enter Registration Code.

2. Enter the name you used to register your copy of WinZip in the Name field and the WinZip registration number you were given in the Registration # field; then click OK, as shown in Figure 2-11.

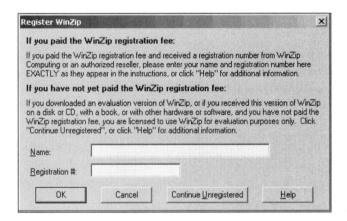

Figure 2-11: Register your copy of WinZip by entering the name you used to register it and the registration number given to you

3. When asked to verify that your WinZip information was recorded correctly, check the information and then click OK.

4. WinZip displays the License Agreement and Warranty Disclaimer dialog box, which you should read. Click View License Agreement to review the terms of your license (Figure 2-12).

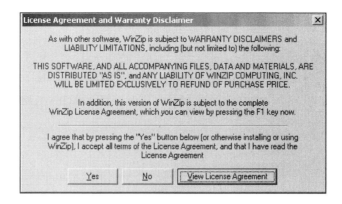

As with other software, WinZip is subject to WARRANTY DISCLAIMERS and LIABILITY LIMITATIONS, including (but not limited to) the following:

THIS SOFTWARE, AND ALL ACCOMPANYING FILES, DATA AND MATERIALS, ARE DISTRIBUTED "AS IS", and ANY LIABILITY OF WINZIP COMPUTING, INC. WILL BE LIMITED EXCLUSIVELY TO REFUND OF PURCHASE PRICE.

In addition, this version of WinZip is subject to the complete WinZip License Agreement, which you can view by pressing the F1 key now.

I agree that by pressing the "Yes" button below (or otherwise installing or using WinZip), I accept all terms of the License Agreement, and that I have read the License Agreement

Figure 2-12: Review the WinZip license agreement before accepting its terms

5. Click Yes to accept the terms of the license and complete the registration process.

From this point onward, you will no longer see the registration reminder| dialog box when you start WinZip.

TIP *To view the name that you used to register your copy of WinZip, as well as your registration number, click the About option in the WinZip Wizard or the About WinZip option on the WinZip Classic Help menu.*

Uninstalling WinZip

To uninstall WinZip from any version of Windows later than Windows 95, use the Add/Remove Programs utility on the Windows Control Panel or click Start • Programs • WinZip • Uninstall WinZip.

NOTE *When you uninstall a registered copy of WinZip, WinZip will display the registered user's name and registration number. If you do not already have this information written down, record it now in case you decide to reinstall WinZip. If you are uninstalling an unregistered trial copy of WinZip, you will not see this dialog box.*

WinZip Technical Support

Unlike many other software companies, WinZip Computing offers free technical support. However, you are strongly encouraged to use WinZip's help system and the Support and FAQs link on the company's main web page before you submit a request for help.

For technical support, email help@winzip.com or click the Support link on the WinZip main web page at www.winzip.com (WinZip Computing's preferred method). Regardless of which of these two support avenues you choose, WinZip Computing asks for the following information:

- Your version of Windows
- The WinZip version you are using
- The exact error message
- Whether you can reproduce the problem
- A list of any other programs running when the error occurred or a description of what you were attempting to do

My experience with WinZip has shown it to be a very reliable application. Most users never experience any problems. However, if you should experience a problem you should make sure that you can reproduce it before you contact WinZip technical support and provide them with as much information as possible.

3

THE WINZIP WIZARD

This chapter introduces you to the WinZip Wizard, which makes common zipping tasks easy. The wizard will step you through the most commonly used WinZip tasks, including the procedures for creating, modifying, and extracting archive contents. Although not as powerful as the WinZip Classic interface, the WinZip Wizard lets you be productive with WinZip right away. Then, once you're comfortable with the basics of using WinZip, you can consider graduating to the WinZip Classic interface.

Organizing Your Download and Archive Files

This chapter shows you how to create, modify, and extract the contents of archives. Archives are files that contain one or more other files, usually in a compressed format. But before you begin, take a moment to consider the best way to store your archives.

As you learned in Chapter 2, WinZip has a built-in feature called Favorite Zip Folders, which allows you to view all of your Zip files in one folder, regardless of where they are stored on your computer. (The Favorite Zip Folders feature is covered in greater detail later in this chapter and in Chapter 4, "Managing Your Archives.")

It's a lot easier to work with WinZip's Favorite Zip Folders feature when you keep your archives in one place, such as in Windows's My Documents folder. Or better yet, why not create a subfolder in the My Documents folder called My Archives and then divide it into several subfolders of its own. For example, consider dividing a My Archives folder into the following subfolders:

My Downloads. Use this folder to temporarily hold all files downloaded from the Internet.

My Uploads. Use this folder to hold all archives you create to email or send over the Internet.

Storage. Use this folder to store archives you're finished with.

Regardless of how you organize your archives, keep their organization simple and manageable so that you can find and use them when you want to.

NOTE *If you use a service like America Online or CompuServe, note where it stores downloads and make sure that you include these folders in your archive management plan. For example, CompuServe typically stores all downloads at C:\cserve\download or some similar location.*

Starting the WinZip Wizard

To start WinZip, choose Start • Programs • WinZip and then click WinZip 8.0 or the WinZip icon on the Start menu. If, when installing, you chose to start the WinZip Wizard by default, WinZip will open with the interface shown in Figure 3-1. Otherwise WinZip will start using the WinZip Classic Interface. However, you can switch to the WinZip Wizard at any time as explained in the next section.

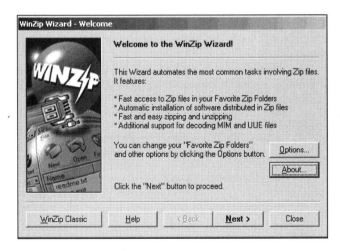

Figure 3-1: The WinZip Wizard provides access to the most commonly performed WinZip tasks

The following options are available in the main WinZip Wizard dialog box:

WinZip Classic. Switches to the more advanced WinZip Classic interface.

Help. Starts WinZip's help.

Next. Begins the archive management process.

Close. Terminates the WinZip Wizard interface (and allows you to change your default startup option for the next time you launch WinZip).

Options. Displays the WinZip Options dialog box, where you can configure various WinZip settings such as your favorite WinZip folders and default unzip folder.

About. Displays information about WinZip, including ordering, license, and system information, as well as a link to FAQs (frequently asked questions) about WinZip.

Switching to WinZip Classic

To switch to WinZip Classic, click the WinZip Classic button shown in Figure 3-1. You might want to use WinZip Classic to perform a task that is not available from the WinZip Wizard, such as:

• Configuring support for external programs

• Creating a self-executing Zip file

• Testing an archive

• Adding a comment to an archive

To switch back to the WinZip Wizard from WinZip Classic, click the Wizard icon, shown in Figure 3-2, on the WinZip Classic toolbar at the top of the screen.

Figure 3-2: Click the Wizard icon on the WinZip Classic toolbar to switch back to the WinZip Wizard

TIP *You can also switch from WinZip Classic to the WinZip Wizard by selecting the Wizard option on the WinZip Classic File menu.*

Using WinZip Help

WinZip has a detailed help system with instructions for performing most WinZip tasks, which you can access from the WinZip Wizard by clicking the Help button shown in Figure 3-1. WinZip help displays help for the WinZip Wizard, as shown in Figure 3-3.

Figure 3-3: WinZip help

The bottom of the help screen has a list of links to commonly requested
information. The help system's toolbar at the top of the screen gives further
access to WinZip help content: Contents brings you back to this main page;
Index brings you to a searchable index of help topics (see Figure 3-4). Browse the
index by typing a few letters of the topic you are looking for in the text box on
the Index tab, or click the Find tab for a more thorough search of help topics.

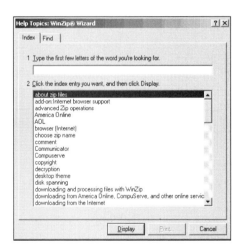

Figure 3-4: Browse WinZip help using Index or do a more thorough search with Find

Back returns you to the previously viewed help topic, and Print lets you print
the topic. Close closes WinZip help, and the << and >> buttons move you forward
and backward through the various pages of information in WinZip help.

If you think you might need to revisit a help topic, you can bookmark it by choosing Bookmark • Define from WinZip help's main menu. Enter a descriptive name for the bookmark you are creating and then click OK. To be sure that your bookmark was saved, choose the Bookmark menu; you should see your bookmark listed just below Define.

Working with Archives

Before you can work with files stored in an archive, you must extract them. When you *extract* a file stored in an archive, you uncompress it and copy the uncompressed file to a particular location, which could be your hard disk, a floppy disk, or someplace on your network. (The original archive remains unchanged.)

Once a file has been extracted, it's exactly as it was before it was compressed, and you can treat it as you normally would. For example, if the file is a program, you can run it; if it is a text file, you can open it in your word processor and work with it. You won't see any sign that it was ever compressed.

To begin working with a file archive, click Next on the WinZip Wizard opening screen (Figure 3-1). This opens the WinZip Wizard – Select Activity screen, where you can do the following:

Unzip or install from an existing Zip file. Steps you through the process for extracting and saving the contents of a Zip file.

Update an existing Zip file. Steps you through the process for adding files to an existing Zip file.

Create a new Zip file. Steps you through the process for creating a new Zip file.

Creating a Zip File

Any time you have more than a couple of files to email or one or more large files to send over a network such as the Internet, consider sending the files as a Zip file. When you do, you'll not only lighten the load on your network, but you'll also spend less time waiting to send your email or upload your files.

To create a new Zip file, follow these steps:

1. Open WinZip and choose Create a new Zip file. The wizard will prompt you for the name you want to use for your new Zip file, as shown in Figure 3-5. To tell WinZip where to place the zipped file, if other than the default location, enter the complete path information along with the file name in the File name field, or click Browse and specify the location and file name.

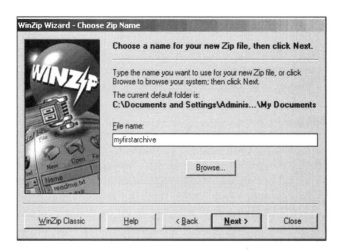

Figure 3-5: Provide a custom name for the archive with the wizard

2. Click Next, and on the following screen select the files or folders to add to the Zip file by clicking Add files or Add folders, as shown in Figure 3-6.

Figure 3-6: The wizard asks you to specify the files and folders to add to the new Zip file

3. Once you've selected the files for your archive, click Zip Now. The wizard will create the new Zip file with the specified files or folders and then offer to create a blank email and attach the newly modified Zip file to it. Click Next. The Wizard then redisplays the options for creating, updating and unzipping archives.

TIP *You can also create a new archive by right-clicking any file or folder and selecting the Add to Zip option on the menu that appears. This opens the WinZip Add box, where you can specify the name of the archive and where you want to create it.*

Extracting Archive Contents

It's just as easy to extract the contents of Zip files as it is to create or update them. To extract the contents of a Zip file, follow these steps:

1. Select "Unzip or install from an existing Zip file" to begin the extraction. The wizard will display a list of all Zip files managed as favorite WinZip folders, as shown in Figure 3-7.

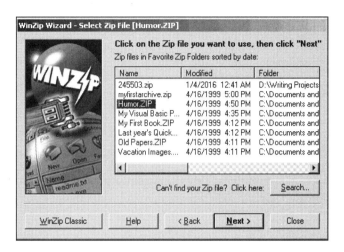

Figure 3-7: The WinZip Wizard lists all Zip files stored in your Favorite Zip Folders collection

If the archive you are looking for is not listed here, click Search to find the folder that contains it and add the folder to the listing. Four search options are available:

Search hard disk(s) on this PC. Searches all disks on the local computer and displays a list of all Zip files found.

Search Favorite Zip Folders. Searches for Zip files in the folders in your Favorite Zip Folders collection.

Search disk. Searches for Zip files on the disk you specify and displays a list of all Zip files found.

Let me find it. Lets you browse your computer and specify the location of the Zip file.

2. To unzip a listed archive, select it and then click Next. WinZip asks you to specify the options to use when extracting an archive's contents, as shown in Figure 3-8.

These extraction options are available:

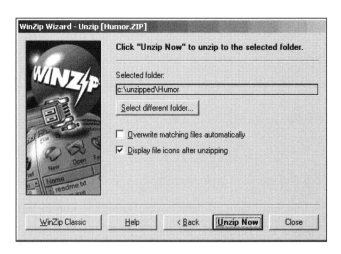

Figure 3-8: You can override default options and specify how and where you want the archive's contents extracted

Select different folder. Lets you specify the folder where you want to store the contents of the Zip file once they are extracted.

WinZip will choose a location for the unzipped file, shown in the Selected folder box. To select a different destination, click the Select different folder option and choose a new location for the unzipped file by either typing it in or browsing to it.

Overwrite matching files automatically. Tells the wizard to overwrite any files with matching files names in the destination folder without asking for confirmation.

To overwrite files in the target folder with the same name as the file that you are uncompressing, select the Overwrite matching files automatically option. Otherwise, WinZip will ask you what to do if it finds a file with the same name in the target directory.

Display file icons after unzipping. Opens an Windows Explorer dialog box showing the contents of the destination folder immediately after extracting the archive's contents.

The Display file icons after unzipping option tells WinZip to open a Windows Explorer window to show the extracted files once it's finished decompressing them (as shown in Figure 3-9).

3. Click Unzip Now to extract the file. When it finishes, the wizard will summarize the results of the extraction and let you know if there were any errors. Click Next to extract another file, or click Close to exit.

TIP *You can open any Zip file by double-clicking it. This will start WinZip and load the archive so that you can view and extract its contents. (See Chapter 8 for more information on how WinZip integrates with Windows to provide quick access to your Zip files.)*

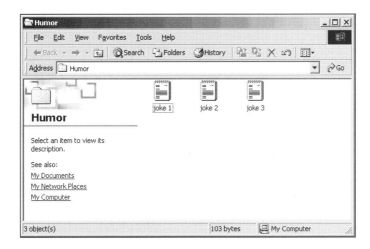

Figure 3-9: WinZip opens a Windows Explorer window and displays extracted files

Adding Files to an Archive

It's easy to add a file to an existing Zip archive without having to recompress everything all over again. This feature will come in handy when you receive a Zip file from someone and need to modify its contents and return it, or if you're storing files in an archive that you are continually adding to.

To add a file to an existing archive, follow these steps:

1. Start the WinZip Wizard, choose Next, and then choose Update an existing Zip file. The wizard displays a list of all Zip files stored in your Favorite Zip Folders collection. (If the archive you are looking for is not listed, click Search to find it.) To update an archive, select it and click Next. You are asked to specify the files or folders you want to add to the selected archive, as shown in Figure 3-10.

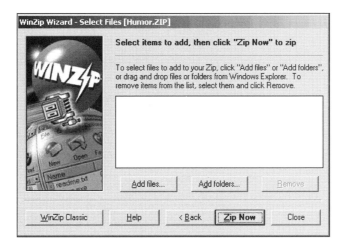

Figure 3-10: Specify the files and folders you want to add to the Zip file

2. Select either the Add files or Add folders option and browse to the files or folders you want to add. Select files or folders by double-clicking them; you can add as many as you want.

3. Once you have selected the items you want to add, click Zip Now, and the wizard will add the items to the archive. You'll also have the option to email your newly modified Zip file, using your default email client, as shown in Figure 3-11. (See Chapter 8, "Operating System Integration," for more information on WinZip's Zip and Mail feature.) For now, click Next to return to the main activity screen.

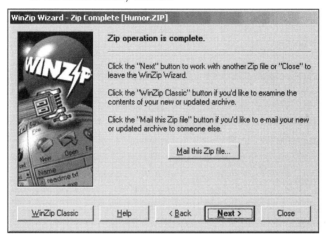

Figure 3-11: The wizard will offer to email your newly modified Zip file

TIP *To add more files and folders to any Zip file, drag and drop them onto an archive. This will open the WinZip Add dialog box, where you can specify the name of the archive you want to modify.*

Disk Spanning

Disk spanning is a technique used to store a large archive across multiple removable disks such as floppy disks. You can crate a new archive that spans multiple floppy disks by simply specifying the floppy disk drive as the destination for the archive and clicking Zip Now. WinZip will automatically prompt you to insert additional diskettes when required, as shown in Figure 3-12, thus spanning the archive over several floppies.

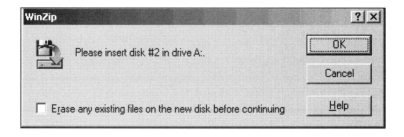

Figure 3-12: Create an archive that spans multiple floppies

NOTE *Disk spanning works only when creating a new Zip file from scratch. You cannot use it to span an existing Zip file, nor can you add a new file to an existing Zip file and then span it.*

Configuring WinZip Options

The WinZip Wizard provides access to a limited set of options that you can configure to control WinZip operations. View and change these settings by clicking the Options button on the WinZip Wizard opening screen.

The Favorite Zip Folders tab, shown in Figure 3-13, displays a list of favorite WinZip folders. If a particular folder containing Zip files is absent from this list, you can add it by clicking Add a folder to list and then specifying the folder's location. Remove a folder by selecting it and clicking Remove folder.

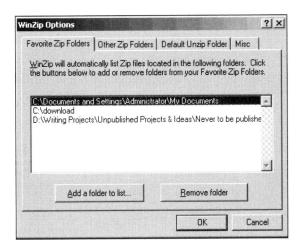

Figure 3-13: Use the WinZip Options dialog box to view, add, or delete favorite Zip folders

The Other Zip Folders tab, shown in Figure 3-14, tells WinZip what to do when you find a Zip file in a folder that is not already listed as one of your favorites. You have three options:

- Add the folder to the Favorite Zip Folders automatically
- Ask before adding the folder to the Favorite Zip Folders
- Do not add the folder to the Favorite Zip Folders.

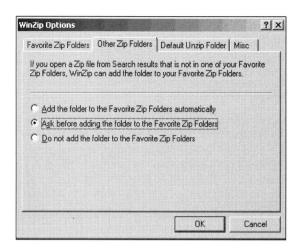

Figure 3-14: The wizard lets you decide when WinZip will ask you to add folders to the Favorite Zip Folders collection

The Default UnZip Folder tab, shown in Figure 3-15, specifies WinZip's default folder used in unzip operations. To change the default, c:\unzipped, click Browse and select a new folder.

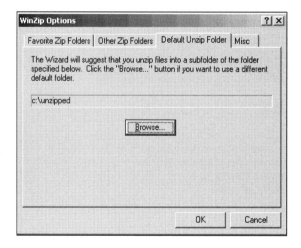

Figure 3-15: Use the wizard to choose the default folder where WinZip extracts all archives

The Misc tab, shown in Figure 3-16, configures several WinZip settings. Its top portion specifies interface settings, including whether to start with the wizard or WinZip Classic. (You can choose only one option here.) You can also decide here whether WinZip will display the Switch Interface dialog box (discussed later in this section) when you start with WinZip Classic and then switch to the wizard and close WinZip, or vice versa. (This option is on by default; clear it if you don't want to see this dialog box when closing WinZip.)

If you enable the WinZip 7.0-compatible wizard (no Update or Create) option, WinZip will display a WinZip version 7 wizard interface. WinZip version 7 and earlier versions of WinZip do not support the creation or modification of Zip files from the WinZip Wizard. The advantage of enabling this option is that is helps to streamline the wizard's functionality if you intend to use WinZip only to unzip and manage archives, by eliminating the WinZip - Select Activity box.

The Enable desktop theme/screen saver installer option determines whether WinZip can install Windows themes and screen savers contained in archives. If you disable this option, you will have to manually install your new themes and screen savers.

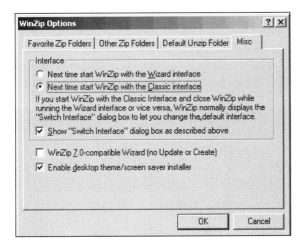

Figure 3-16: The WinZip Wizard provides access to a subset of WinZip's configuration options

Selecting Your Default WinZip Interface

The WinZip – Switch Interface dialog box, shown in Figure 3-17, appears any time you start WinZip using one WinZip's interface (such as WinZip Wizard) and then close it after switching to the other user interface (WinZip Classic).

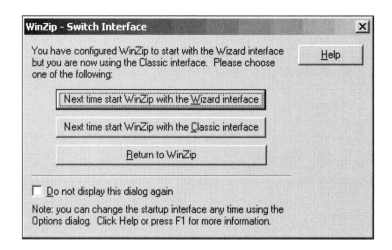

Figure 3-17: Whenever you start WinZip with one interface and then close it while using the other interface, WinZip prompts you to specify which interface you want to set as your default

If you started WinZip using the Classic interface and want to start it the next time using the wizard, select Next time start WinZip with the Wizard interface, or vice versa. WinZip waits for you to select an option before closing. To avoid having to make this choice, you can click Return to WinZip, continue working, and then switch back to the original user interface before closing. You can also select Do not display this dialog again to eliminate this question forever.

TIP *If you select the Do not display this dialog again option and later change your mind, you can reenable the dialog box from the WinZip Wizard by clicking Options and then selecting the Show "Switch Interface" dialog box option on the Misc tab.*

4

MANAGING YOUR ARCHIVES

This is the first of two chapters with detailed coverage of WinZip Classic, the advanced WinZip user interface. WinZip Classic lets you do everything you can do with the WinZip Wizard, but also includes lots of additional features.

This chapter shows you how to create Zip files using WinZip classic and how to use several options not available through the wizard, including the option to view archive properties and contents before unzipping them. You'll also learn several new ways to work with your archives, including ways to copy, move, delete, and rename them.

The WinZip Classic Window

The WinZip Classic interface, shown with labels in Figure 4-1, is WinZip's advanced user interface, offering every available feature. From this screen, you can click toolbar buttons or select menu options to do all your work.

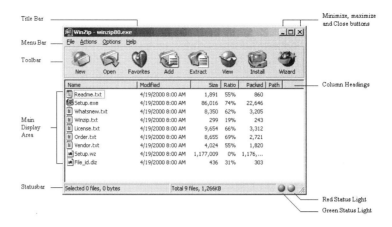

Figure 4-1: The WinZip Classic interface is designed for more experienced WinZip users

WinZip Classic works much like any Windows application. The WinZip title bar at the top of the screen shows the name of the currently opened archive. The Minimize, Maximize, and Close buttons on the right side of the title bar let you control the size of the WinZip screen and close the application.

The WinZip menu bar beneath the title bar contains the following menus:

File. Provides access to submenus that allow you to work with the entire archive.

Actions. Provides access to submenus that allow you to work with one or more files in an archive.

Options. Provides access to submenus that you can use to configure WinZip.

Help. Use this menu to get help and learn more about WinZip.

Although the WinZip menu bar provides access to all WinZip functionality, the functions available are context sensitive. For example, the submenu options on the Actions menu affect only open archives, so they are available only when an archive is opened.

The WinZip toolbar (Figure 4-2) provides easy access to commonly used WinZip features.

Figure 4-2: The WinZip toolbar provides single-click access to commonly used WinZip features

As you will learn in Chapter 6, "WinZip Classic Configuration Options," the WinZip toolbar is highly configurable, allowing you to add and remove WinZip buttons to include the WinZip features that you use most often.

By default, the WinZip toolbar contains these functions:

New. Opens the New Archive screen, where you can create a new archive.

Open. Opens the Open Archive screen, where you can select an archive to work with.

Favorites. Opens the Favorite Zip Folders screen, where you can manage all your archives.

Add. Opens the Add screen, where you can add files to your existing archives.

Extract. Opens the Extract screen that you use to unzip the contents of an archive.

View. Opens the View screen, where you preview an archive file.

Install. Opens the Install screen, where you can run setup programs and install desktop and screen saver files contained in your archives.

Wizard. Switches to WinZip Wizard.

Figure 4-3: The WinZip Internet Explorer-like toolbar

WinZip also provides an optional Internet Explorer-like toolbar, shown in Figure 4-3, which you can use in place of the default toolbar, shown in Figure 4-2. To use it, right-click the toolbar and choose Explorer-Style Buttons.

Beneath the WinZip toolbar are a series of column headings. These headings indicate various types of information about each archive, such as the name and size.

The status bar at the bottom of the WinZip screen (see Figure 4-1) consists of several sections. On the left side, WinZip displays the number of currently selected archive files and their combined size. In the middle, it shows the total number of files in the archive and their combined size. The right side of the status bar displays red and green status lights. The green light is on when WinZip is idle and ready for work; the red light is on when WinZip is busy performing a task such as zipping or unzipping an archive.

Creating a New Archive

To create your own Zip file or to add a group of files to a single archive, follow these steps:

1. Choose File • New Archive or click the New button on the WinZip toolbar. The New Archive dialog box appears, as shown in Figure 4-4.

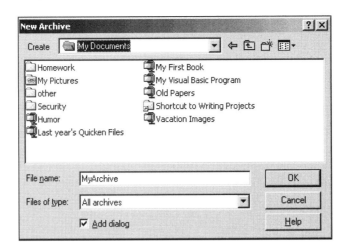

Figure 4-4: Naming a new Zip file

2. Enter a name for the Zip file in the File name field. Then, in the Create box (shown at the top of Figure 4-4), browse to the location where you want to store the file. Make sure that the Add dialog option at the bottom of the screen is checked; then click OK. The Add screen appears, as shown in Figure 4-5.

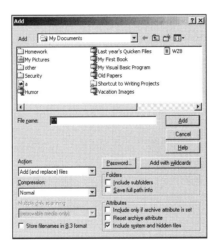

Figure 4-5: Selecting files to add to the new archive

NOTE *When the Add dialog option is selected (the default choice), WinZip automatically displays the Add screen so that you can select the files you want to copy to the archive. If you clear this selection, WinZip creates an empty Zip file.*

3. Use the Add drop-down list (shown at the top of Figure 4-5) to locate the folder where the files you want to add to the archive are stored. Then select one or more files to add, or enter the name of the file to be added in the File name field.

You can use wildcard characters to add more than one file at a time when entering a file name in the File name field. A wildcard is a character that can be used to represent one or more characters. For example, a question mark (?) can be used to represent a single character, and an asterisk (*) can be used to represent any number of characters. For instance, typing ***.log** *copies all files with a .log file extension to the Zip file.*

4. Choose any options you want at the bottom of the screen; then click Add to create the new Zip file. WinZip displays the new Zip file and its file contents as shown in Figure 4-6. Detailed information on what these options do is provided later in this chapter.

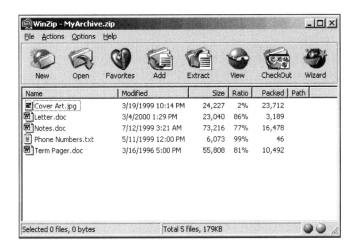

Figure 4-6: Viewing the contents of the new Zip file

The first two columns show the names of files stored in the archive and when they were last modified. The third column lists each file's normal uncompressed size. The Ratio column tells you how much WinZip was able to reduce the size of each file, and the Packed column shows the size of the file as stored in the archive.

Examining the New Archive

The archive we've created in this example consists of five files, as shown in Figure 4-6. As you can see in the Ratio column, WinZip's ability to compress these files varied greatly. For example, it was able to reduce the size of the Cover Art.jpg graphic file by only 2 percent (JPEG graphics are already compressed). On the other hand, the three Microsoft Word files (Letter.doc, Notes.doc, and Term Pager.doc) were compressed an average of about 80 percent, and Phone Numbers.txt by 99%.

Fine-Tuning the Zip File Creation Process

WinZip provides a number of optional configuration parameters that you can set when creating a new archive. You can use these options to control WinZip's behavior when creating an archive or to customize many of the characteristics of your Zip files.

Controlling WinZip's Behavior

The first configuration option on the Add screen is the Action setting, which is specified by selecting an option from a drop-down selection list, as shown in Figure 4-7.

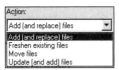

Figure 4-7: Telling WinZip Classic how to behave when adding files to an archive

The options for this setting are as follows:

Add (and replace) files. Adds all selected files to the new archive.

Freshen existing files. Updates files in an existing archive if file versions have changed, but does not add any new files. Use this option to update the files already stored in an archive. Because this option replaces existing files in the archive with the updated ones, proceed with caution.

Move files. Adds files to an existing archive and deletes the originals.

Update (and add) files. This option does the same thing as the first two options combined. It updates files in an existing archive and adds new files. Use this option to update the files already stored in an archive or to add new files to the archive.

Setting the Compression Ratio

You can provide WinZip with guidelines for determining the size and compression ratio of archived files by selecting one of the options in the Compression drop-down list, shown in Figure 4-8.

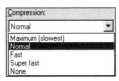

Figure 4-8: Setting the compression ratio for your Zip files

Your compression options follow. Faster options usually produce larger Zip files, but the files compress and uncompress more quickly.

Maximum (slowest). Creates the smallest possible Zip file. This option takes the longest to run, and archives created with it will take slightly longer to unzip. For example, you might use this option to shrink a Zip file to make it small enough to fit on a floppy disk.

Normal. Creates a Zip file using WinZip's default level of compression. This option balances the need for file compression with the amount of time it takes to unzip an archive.

Fast. Creates Zip files that are slightly larger than ones created using the normal compression setting and that unzip slightly faster.

Super fast. Creates archives using WinZip's minimal compression setting and that unzip quickly.

None. Groups files into an archive without compressing them.

Storing Zip Files Across Multiple Floppy Disks

WinZip allows you to store your archives on floppy disks or other types of removable media by allowing you to specify the drive where you want to create your archive. However, sometimes your archives may be larger than your floppy disks can hold (1.44MB).

If your archive won't fit on a single floppy disk, re-create the Zip file using the maximum compression setting and see if that shrinks the archive enough for it to fit. If not, consider using disk spanning. As you learned in Chapter 3, "The WinZip Wizard," disk spanning allows WinZip to store a Zip file across multiple floppy disks.

However, disk spanning does have its limitations. For one, WinZip allows you to use it only when creating a new archive. Also, when unzipping the contents of a Zip file that spans multiple disks, you lose the ability to extract individual files.

NOTE   *To use WinZip's disk spanning capability, you will need preformatted disks available. WinZip will not format the disks for you.*

WinZip provides several options for configuring the disk spanning feature, as shown in Figure 4-9. You'll find these options on the Add screen, just below the compression options.

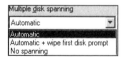

Figure 4-9: Enabling multiple-disk spanning

When using disk spanning, these are your options:

Automatic. Lets WinZip span as required.

Automatic + wipe first disk prompt. Tells WinZip to prompt you to erase all files on the destination disks before copying your archive files to them.

No spanning. Disables disk spanning.

Saving Zip Files Using Old-Style MS-DOS Names

Before the advent of Windows 95, all Windows operating systems were limited to file names of 8 or fewer characters plus an optional three-character file extension. Windows 95 and all subsequent versions of Windows support file names up to 256 characters long, also known as long file names. By default, WinZip allows you to create archives that use long file names. However, if you plan on working with your Zip files on a computer running Windows 3.1, which does not support long file names, you should create files with names that are fewer than 8 characters long. If you prefer to keep working with long file names but still want to make files accessible to older Windows computers, you can configure WinZip to automatically convert the names of any files that you add to an archive to the 8.3 character format by selecting the Store filenames in 8.3 format setting.

Securing Your Archives

To keep your archives private, you can encrypt them and protect them with a password. Once password protected, your files can be opened only by entering the password used to encrypt the file.

You can encrypt your archive when your create it by clicking the Add screen's Password button. The Password screen then appears, as shown in Figure 4-10.

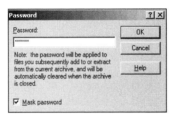

Figure 4-10: Password protecting your Zip file

The Password screen's only option, Mask password (on by default), hides the characters that you type in the Password field from prying eyes. When enabled, Mask password asks you to type your password twice to make sure you did not make a typo the first time. (When this option is disabled, your password is visible as you type it, so you don't need to confirm it.)

NOTE *Don't be lulled into a false sense of security just because you have encrypted your Zip file. Several free programs on the Internet will let anyone decrypt your password-protected Zip file. However, most people are unaware of these programs and won't know what to do when they encounter an encrypted Zip file. As an alternative to using WinZip built-in encryption, check out some of the encryption utilities available at most shareware sites (such as download.com) that use stronger encryption technologies. (Search under encryption.)*

Adding Multiple Files to Your New Archive

Click the Add with wildcards button to add multiple files to the new archive using wildcard characters, which you enter in the File name field. For example, if you have a collection of jpeg (.jpg) image files of your family that you want to store, you might enter ***.jpg** and click Add with wildcards to add all image files in the current folder to the archive. Alternatively, you could use the question mark character to match files using single-character pattern matching. For example, you might enter **10-0?-01.jpg** in the File name field and click Add with wildcards to match all image files that you downloaded from your digital camera during the first nine days in October 2001.

Configuring Folder Options

WinZip provides two options on the Add screen for controlling how it deals with folders when creating a new archive. The first, Include subfolders, tells WinZip to add all files in the current folder and all of its subfolders. If this option is not selected, WinZip will add files only in the current folder. The second option, Save full path info, tells WinZip to save the path information of all files stored in the archive. This second option is particularly useful when you want to send someone a collection of files that will maintain their original folder structure when unzipped, rather than all being grouped into one folder.

For example, say you write a lot of letters and store them on your computer in a folder called MyLetters. To help keep things better organized as the number of letters you write grows, you might further organize your letters into subfolders inside the MyLetters folder. For example, you might have subfolders named Mom, Bank, Taxes, and Orders. To create an archive of all of your letters, you might find it handy to also save their folder structure. In this way, when you unzip your archive on another computer, you can have WinZip re-create your original folder structure and then unzip your letters into their original folders.

Working with File Attributes

The Windows operating system supports five file attributes that describe various properties of a file. They are Read-only, Hidden, Archive, System, and Compression. A detailed discussion of these attributes is beyond the scope of this book, but suffice it to say that file attributes can be used to affect the behavior of a file. For example, turning a file's read-only attribute on prevents the file from being deleted without first turning this attribute off.

The three options in the Attributes section of the Add screen are as follows:

Include only if archive attribute is set. Tells WinZip to ignore files that do not have their archive attribute set. The archive attribute is usually used by backup programs to identify files that have changed since the last backup and which need to be backed up.

Reset archive attribute. Tells WinZip to clear the file archive attribute after adding the files to a Zip file.

Include system and hidden files. This, the default setting, tells WinZip to copy all files, including hidden and system files. Hidden files are files that have been set so that they do not appear when you use Windows Explorer or other programs to view the folder that contains them. Applications often mark files as hidden to prevent their accidental deletion or modification. System files are files that are critical to the proper functioning of the operating system.

Opening and Viewing Archive Contents

Now that you have created your first Zip file, let's open it to see how things turned out. To do so, follow these steps:

1. Select Open Archive from the WinZip File menu, as shown in Figure 4-11. WinZip opens the Open Archive screen so that you can find and select your archive.

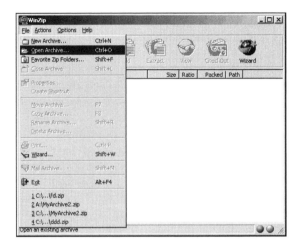

Figure 4-11: Opening an archive

2. Use the Look in drop-down box to specify the location of the archive file, as shown in Figure 4-12.

Figure 4-12: Use the Look in drop-down box to locate and select your Zip file

By default, the Files of type field displays the entry All files (*.*), which shows all files in the current folder. To limit the number of files displayed, you can filter them by type using these options:

Zip files. Displays only Zip files.

All archives. Displays all archive files supported by WinZip, such as files with .zip, .tar, and .cab extensions.

Encoded files. Displays only encoded files such as those used by older email systems that require all nontext files to be encoded or converted to text before delivery. Examples of these file types include files with .uu and .uue file extension.

Archives and .exe files. Displays all archives and all executable files (files with an .exe extension).

Archives, encoded files, and .exe files. Display all archive files, all encoded files, and all executable files.

All files (*.*). Display all files.

Once you've made your selection, click Open, and WinZip will open your archive and display its contents, as explained in the next section.

Viewing Archive Contents

When you open an archive, WinZip displays detailed information about its files, as shown in Figure 4-13. The Name column lists each file's name. The remaining columns display the following information:

Modified. Lists the date and time that the file was last created or modified.

Size. Shows the size of the uncompressed file.

Ratio. Shows the extent to which the file has been compressed.

Packed. Shows the size of the compressed file inside the archive.

Path. Shows the path of the file on the system where the archive was created (if available). For example, if you archived all the image files in your c:\MyPics folder, the path would be c:\MyPics. This information is available only if the Save full path info option on the Add screen was selected when the Zip file was created.

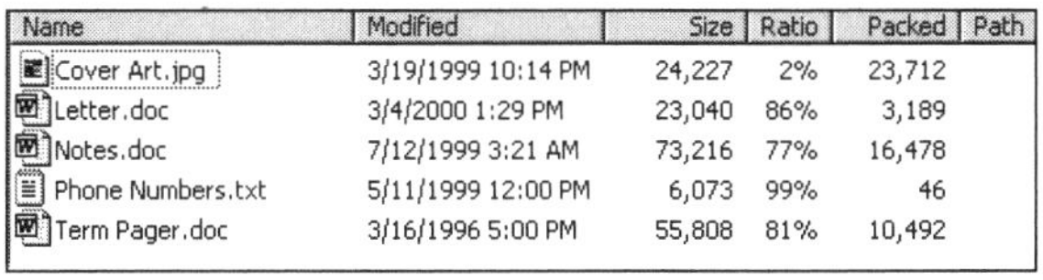

Name	Modified	Size	Ratio	Packed	Path
Cover Art.jpg	3/19/1999 10:14 PM	24,227	2%	23,712	
Letter.doc	3/4/2000 1:29 PM	23,040	86%	3,189	
Notes.doc	7/12/1999 3:21 AM	73,216	77%	16,478	
Phone Numbers.txt	5/11/1999 12:00 PM	6,073	99%	46	
Term Pager.doc	3/16/1996 5:00 PM	55,808	81%	10,492	

Figure 4-13: WinZip displays detailed information about each file in the archive

By default, the archive's listing is sorted by file name in ascending order, but you can change the sort order by clicking each column heading. When you do, a blue arrow appears in the selected column, as shown in Figure 4-14, and the files in the archive are sorted based on the selected column. In this example, the archive is sorted based on the last modification date of each file. Click a column heading again to reverse the sort order.

Figure 4-14: Sorting the Zip file's contents by file modification date

Working with the Favorite Zip Folders Feature

WinZip's Favorite Zip Folders feature helps track your archives by keeping an eye on the folders that contain them. To view the Favorite Zip Folders screen, shown in Figure 4-15, select the Favorite Zip Folders option on the File menu or click the Favorites icon on the WinZip toolbar.

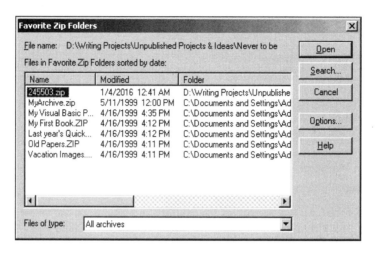

Figure 4-15: Viewing WinZip's Favorite Zip Folders screen

By default, the Favorite Zip Folders screen shows all archives in all monitored folders. You can filter this display by changing the value of the Files of type drop-down list at the bottom of the screen:

Zip files. Displays only Zip files.

All archives. Displays all archives. This is the default setting.

Encoded files. Displays only encoded file.

To view an archive, select it and click the Open button. Click the Search button to tell WinZip to look for new archives, or click the Options button to configure the way that WinZip handles your Favorites folders. (Both of these options are explained in detail in Chapter 3, "The WinZip Wizard.")

Viewing an Archive's Properties

You can learn many things about an archive by examining its properties. For example, if you have two copies of an archive and want to know which is the older copy, you can check each archive's properties and see the date and time that each archive was last created or updated.

To view an archive's properties, open the archive and then choose File •
Properties. The ZIP Properties dialog box appears, as shown in Figure 4-16.

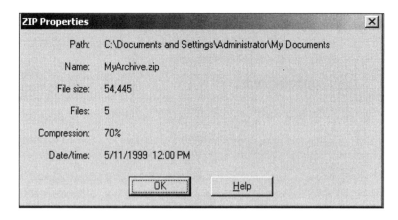

Figure 4-16: Viewing archive properties

The following information is available here:

Path. Displays the path to the archive on the computer where the archive
resides. For example, the Path property shown in Figure 4-16 shows that the
archive resides in C:\Documents and Settings\Administrator\My Documents.

Name. Displays the archive's name.

File size. Displays the archive's file size in bytes.

Files. Lists the number of files in the archive.

Compression. Shows the archive's level of compression.

Date/time. Shows the date and time that the archive was created or last updated.

Click OK to close the ZIP Properties dialog box and return to WinZip Classic.

Creating an Archive Shortcut

WinZip makes it easier to open your archives by helping you add a shortcut to
them on your desktop. To create a shortcut, open an archive in WinZip and
select File • Create Shortcut, and you're done. You should now have a shortcut
on your desktop to the archive, and the next time you want to work with that
archive, you can double-click the shortcut to open the archive automatically.

Using Keyboard Shortcuts

If you prefer the keyboard to the mouse, you may want to use WinZip's keyboard
shortcuts when working in WinZip Classic. Keyboard shortcuts are key combinations that you use to execute WinZip operations. For example, press CTRL+O

(which means press and hold the Control key and then press the letter O) to open an archive.

The available keyboard shortcuts are listed on the WinZip Classic menus. For example, Figure 4-17 shows the shortcuts from the File menu, with the shortcuts to the right of each menu option. (As you can see, not every operation has a keyboard shortcut, though most do.)

Figure 4-17: WinZip's keystroke shortcuts

NOTE *Keyboard shortcuts are available only when you are working in the WinZip Classic interface. The WinZip Wizard does not support them.*

Other Archive Management Operations

WinZip provides a number of additional features for managing your archives, including the ability to copy or move your archives and to rename or delete them. The following sections cover these options.

Moving an Archive

To move an archive using WinZip Classic, open the archive and then choose File • Move archive or press F7. The Move screen (shown in Figure 4-18) lets you enter the location to which you want to move the archive or browse to the location. Once you've entered the location, click OK, and WinZip will copy the archive to the new location and delete it from its current one.

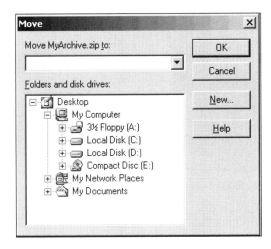

Figure 4-18: Moving an archive to a different location

Copying an Archive

Copying a file works like moving an archive except that WinZip does not delete the original file once the copy operation is complete. To copy an archive, open it and choose File • Copy or press F8. Then specify the location where you want the copy placed.

Renaming an Archive

To rename an open archive in WinZip classic, select File • Rename Archive or press SHIFT+R. Then rename your archive in the To field and click OK, as shown in Figure 4-19.

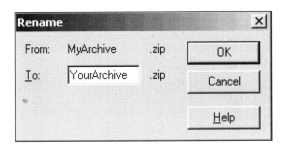

Figure 4-19: Renaming your archive

Deleting an Archive

To delete an open archive in WinZip Classic, select File • Delete Archive and then confirm your request to delete the archive, as shown in Figure 4-20. Once you click Yes, WinZip closes the open archive and deletes it.

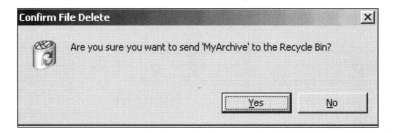

Figure 4-20: Deleting your archive

Printing Archive Contents

To print a list of an archive's contents, choose File • Print or press CTRL+P. To print the report, click OK, as shown in Figure 4-21.

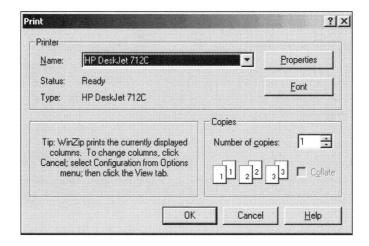

Figure 4-21: Printing an archive report

Here's what a typical WinZip archive report might look like:

```
11/20/01  3:36 PM   C:\Mydocs\xxx\MyArchive.zip              Page 1


Name             Modified            Size  Ratio  Packed  Path
Accounts.doc     11/20/01 3:23 PM     268   43%     153
Appointments.txt 11/20/01 3:33 PM  59,774   99%     387
Contacts.txt     11/20/01 3:34 PM  39,248   99%     272
Forecast.xls     11/20/01 3:35 PM  15,360   84%   2,440
4 file(s)                         114,650   97%   3,252
```

Emailing an Archive

As you saw in Chapter 3, "The WinZip Wizard," the WinZip Wizard makes emailing your archives a snap. This feature is also supported by WinZip Classic. To zip and mail from WinZip Classic, open your archive and choose File • Mail Archive. WinZip should automatically open your email program and attach the archive to a new message, as shown in Figure 4-22. All you need to do is address and send the message.

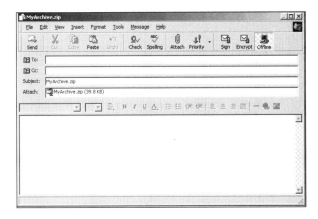

Figure 4-22: Attaching an archive to a new message

Opening a Recently Accessed Archive

WinZip provides a speedy way for you to find and open recently used archives by maintaining a list of the last few archives that you have worked with and displaying it at the bottom of the File menu, as shown in Figure 4-23. Select any archive in that list to open it.

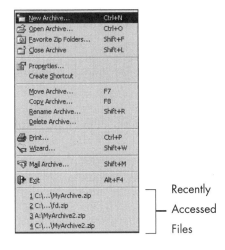

Figure 4-23: Opening a recently accessed archive

5

WORKING WITH THE FILES IN YOUR ARCHIVES

This is the second of two chapters with detailed coverage of WinZip Classic. Whereas Chapter 4 covered features for creating, copying, moving, and deleting entire archives, this chapter shows you how to work with the individual files in your archives.

You'll learn how to unzip one or several files from an archive, how to add one or more files to existing archives, and how to preview individual archive files before opening them. You'll even learn how to open files straight from the archive, modify them, and then update the archive with the modified file.

Adding Files to an Existing Zip File

If you have a Zip file with files that need frequent updating, or if you simply need to add a few more files to a Zip file before sending it to a friend, you can do so using the WinZip Add option as shown in the following procedure. This option is the same as the WinZip Wizard's Update an existing Zip file option, covered in Chapter 3, "The WinZip Wizard."

This option works only with Zip archives and not with other archive file types.

1. Open an existing Zip file using WinZip Classic.

2. Click the Add option on the WinZip Actions menu or the Add button on the WinZip toolbar. The Add screen appears.

3. Using the Add from drop-down list at the top of the screen, locate the file or files that you want to add to the Zip file.

4. Click the appropriate selection in the Action drop-down list at the bottom left of the screen to determine how WinZip will handle the update operations, as shown in Figure 5-1. The available options are as follows:

   Add (and replace) files. Adds new files and replaces any files in the archive with duplicate file names.

   Freshen existing files. Replaces or updates files in the archive without adding any new files to the archive. This option can be used to update the files in your archives and ensure that they remain current.

   Move files. Copies the specified files into the Zip file and then deletes them. This option reduces your overall storage requirements by ensuring that only the copies of files located in Zip files remain on your computer.

   Update (and add) files. Replaces any duplicate files and adds any new files.

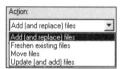

Figure 5-1: Determining WinZip behavior when adding new files to existing Zip files

5. Verify that the rest of the configuration settings on the screen are specified correctly. These are the same settings used when creating a new archive, as covered in Chapter 4, "Managing Your Archive."

6. Click Add. The new file(s) are added to the Zip file and will appear in the file listing on the WinZip Classic screen.

WinZip provides several alternative ways that allow you to quickly add files to Zip files. For example, you can also open Zip files in WinZip and then drag and drop new files onto the WinZip Classic interface. WinZip will automatically add them to the archive. You can also right-click any file and select the Add to Zip option, which lets you specify the Zip file that you want to modify. You can also add new files by dragging and dropping them onto the Zip file icons and clicking Add when prompted.

Deleting Archive Files

To delete a file stored in an archive (thus reducing the size of the archive), open the archive, select the file to delete, and press DELETE. When the Delete screen appears, as shown in Figure 5-2, click the Delete button.

You have a couple of alternatives on the Delete screen: you can type the name of the file you want to delete in the Files field, delete multiple files using wildcard characters, or check the box to delete the entire archive. For example, using wildcard characters you could type ***.jpg** in the Files field and click Delete to remove all JPEG graphic files from the archive.

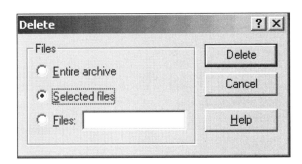

Figure 5-2: Removing files from your archives

 To delete more than one archive file at a time, hold down SHIFT or CTRL when selecting the files. Holding down SHIFT lets you select a range of contiguous files, and holding down CTRL lets you select individual files regardless of their order in the archive.

 WinZip delete operations cannot be undone. If you accidentally delete the wrong file, the only way to replace it is to add it back to the archive (assuming that you still have the original file).

Unzipping Archives

WinZip is most commonly used to unzip or extract the contents of Zip files downloaded from the Internet. Although you can use the WinZip Wizard to do this, WinZip Classic provides more options and is faster, once you're comfortable with it.

Unzipping an Entire Archive

To unzip an entire archive using WinZip Classic, follow these steps:

1. Open the archive and click the Extract icon on the toolbar. The Extract screen appears, as shown in Figure 5-3.

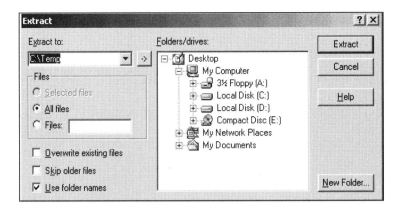

Figure 5-3: Unzipping all the files in an archive

2. Enter or browse to the destination for the unzipped files in the Extract to box. Or click the New Folder button to create a new folder to hold the unzipped archive, as shown in Figure 5-4.

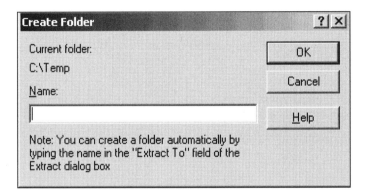

Figure 5-4: Specifying a new folder where you want to unzip the archive

3. To extract all files in the archive, leave the All files option in the Files section selected. To unzip only certain files, enter their names in the Files field (wildcards are okay).

4. Choose any of the following options; then click Extract.

    Overwrite existing files. Tells WinZip to automatically overwrite files with duplicate names in the destination folder. If this option is not selected, WinZip will ask you whether to overwrite each duplicate file that it finds.

Skip older files. Tells WinZip not to overwrite files on disk if they are newer than those in the archive.

Use folder names. Tells WinZip to re-create the files' original directory structure. This option works only if the path information was specified when the Zip file was created. Otherwise, all files are extracted into the current folder. For example, if the files in the archive were located in the C:\Mydocs folder on the original computer when the Zip file was created, and if path information was stored in the Zip file, you can use this option to create a \Mydocs folder on the computer where you are unzipping the archive.

Unzipping Specific Files

In Chapter 3, "The WinZip Wizard," you learned how to unzip entire archives using the wizard interface. Earlier in this chapter, you learned how to perform the same operation using WinZip Classic. However, sometimes you may want to extract only one or two files from an archive. WinZip offers several ways to do so, as detailed in the following sections.

Extracting Selected Files

If you already have the archive open in WinZip Classic and see the files that you want to extract, select the files to extract, and then click Extract. As shown in Figure 5-5, the Files section of the Extract screen will then be set to Selected files. Leave this option as it is; then click Extract to unzip the selected files.

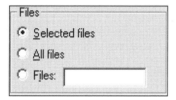

Figure 5-5: Deleting selected files from an archive

Using Drag-and-Drop File Extraction

Using drag and drop, you can extract some or all of the files in an archive. As shown in Figure 5-6, click the files you want to extract and drag them to their new location. (You'll end up with two copies of your files: the compressed versions in your original archive and the uncompressed versions at the new location.)

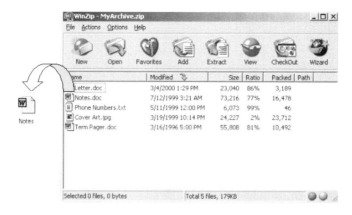

Figure 5-6: Using drag and drop to extract a file from an archive

Viewing Compressed Files Without Unzipping Them

One very convenient WinZip feature is the capability to view individual archive files without extracting them. In fact, WinZip tracks your activity, so if you change the file you were viewing, when you close the file, WinZip will ask if you want to save its modified version back into the archive.

Figure 5-7 shows how WinZip lets you open unzipped files in other Windows applications (in this case, the Windows application is Microsoft Word). In this example, the pointer was placed over the Letter.doc file inside the archive, the mouse button was clicked, and the files were dragged and dropped onto an open Microsoft Word session.

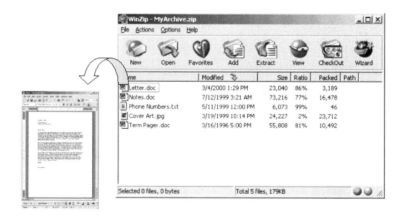

Figure 5-7: Opening an archive file in a Windows application

If you modify a file while viewing it in Microsoft Word, Word will ask you whether to save your changes, and then WinZip will ask you whether you want to add the updated file back into the archive, as shown in Figure 5-8.

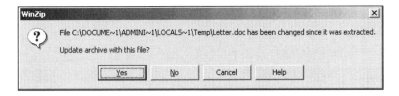

Figure 5-8: Adding a changed file back into its archive

Click Yes to tell WinZip to replace the file stored in the archive with the updated file, or click No to leave the archive as it is. If you click Cancel, WinZip will wait to ask you what to do with the file until you either close the archive or exit WinZip.

In addition to opening an archive file using drag and drop, you can right-click an archive and select Open with WinZip, as shown in Figure 5-9. The file will then be automatically loaded into the application registered in Windows to handle that file type.

Figure 5-9: Opening an archive using the Open with WinZip option

Viewing an Archive File

In addition to opening archive files in other applications without extracting them, you can use other WinZip options to take a sneak peak at an archive's contents to see if it is worth extracting. WinZip provides the following viewing options:

Associated program. Lets you load the archive file using the application that Windows specifies as its default application.

Internal ASCII text viewer. Lets you view text files using WinZip's built-in viewer.

Viewer. Lets you specify another application to be used to view the file.

To preview a file, select it and then click the View option on the Actions menu. The View screen will appear, as shown in Figure 5-10, offering all three viewing options. Select an option and click the View button to preview the file.

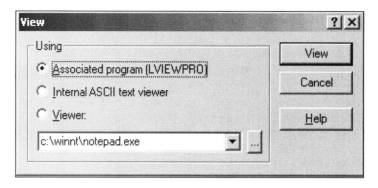

Figure 5-10: Choosing a method for previewing the contents of an archive

NOTE *The Windows quickview.exe program is WinZip's recommended viewer. This is a general-purpose file-viewing application provided by most Windows operating systems. However, Windows 2000 does not provide this program, so this book shows Notepad instead, as shown in Figure 5-10.*

You can also preview a file's contents by right-clicking it and selecting one of the following options:

View. Opens the View screen.

View with internal viewer. Bypasses the View screen and opens the file in WinZip's internal viewer.

View with xxxxxx. Bypasses the View screen and opens the file using the specified viewing application.

Controlling Multiple Archive Files

When you want to work with more than one archive file at a time, WinZip makes it easy to do so with several shortcuts.

For example, you can select any file displayed in WinZip Classic by clicking it; SHIFT-click to select consecutive files, or hold down CTRL while clicking to select multiple files in any order. You can also use the Select All option on the Actions menu to select all files in an archive, or you can deselect all selected files with the Invert Selection option on the same menu.

The WinZip status bar displays information about the files you have selected, including the number of files selected and their combined size. As shown in Figure 5-11, the three files selected have a combined size of 102KB, out of a total of five files in this archive and a total archive size of 179KB.

| Selected 3 files, 102KB | Total 5 files, 179KB |

Figure 5-11: Archive statistics shown on the WinZip status bar

Working with a Virus Scanner

WinZip works with several antivirus programs, including McAfee VirusScan and Norton AntiVirus, to scan the contents of your archives. If you have one of these supported antivirus programs installed on your machine, WinZip should automatically use it to scan your archives. If not, you can manually configure WinZip to use your antivirus program. (See Chapter 6, "WinZip Classic Configuration Options," for more information.)

After WinZip is properly configured, start WinZip's virus scanning by opening an archive and clicking the Virus scan option on the WinZip Actions menu. WinZip will extract the archive contents to a temporary folder, check the files for viruses, and then delete the temporary files and give you the results. If a virus is found, your virus scanner will display a warning message; otherwise, the WinZip message shown in Figure 5-12 will appear.

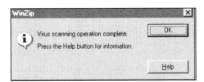

Figure 5-12: WinZip reports that the virus scan has not detected any viruses

NOTE *The WinZip virus scan usually takes place in the background, so you shouldn't see your antivirus program running. However, not all antivirus programs support this option, so you may have to close your antivirus program after it completes its scan.*

Creating a Self-Extracting Archive

If you want to send Zip files to people who may not have an unzipping tool or who may not understand how to work with zipped files, consider making your Zip files self-extracting.

Self-extracting archives are compressed files that automatically extract their contents when opened. Self-extracting archives are very slightly larger than regular Zip files (by about 12KB) because WinZip includes a small, hidden program in the archive that unzips it. (Self-extracting files have an .exe file extension in place of the usual .zip extension.)

Make your Zip files self-extracting as follows:

1. Open the archive that you want to make self-extracting using WinZip Classic.
2. Select the Make .Exe file option from the WinZip Actions menu. WinZip responds by starting the WinZip Self-Extractor Personal Edition, as shown in Figure 5-13.

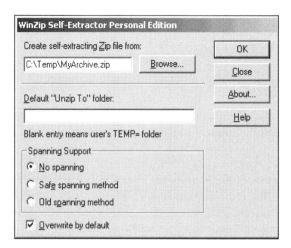

Figure 5-13: The WinZip Self-Extractor Personal Edition screen

3. The archive you will be converting is shown in the box labeled Create self-extracting Zip file from. Specify a different archive by entering the name of a new archive file or by browsing to the archive.

4. Enter a default unzip-to location if you want to set the default unzip-to location for the archive. (Although whoever unzips the archive will be able to override this location, this option offers you the chance to suggest a default folder.)

5. Select the appropriate disk spanning option from the following:

   No spanning. This option displays an "insufficient disk space" message if there is not enough room to create the self-extracting archive and will not extract the archive over multiple floppies.

   Safe spanning method. Use this option to create a self-extracting archive that spans multiple floppies. The first floppy disk in the set will contain two files: the first an executable program that knows how to unzip the archive, and the other a Zip file containing the first part of the archive. The remaining floppy disks in the set will each store a Zip file that together contain the remaining portions of the archive.

   Old spanning method. This option works almost exactly like the Safe spanning method except that the files stored on the second disk and all remaining disks have the .exe file extension instead of the .zip file extension, which may confuse users into thinking that these disks also contain executable programs.

6. If you leave the Overwrite by default option selected (recommended), the self-extracting archive will automatically overwrite files with duplicate file names in the destination folder.

7. Click OK. WinZip Self-Extractor Personal Edition creates the new archive and displays the message shown in Figure 5-14 advising you to test your archive.

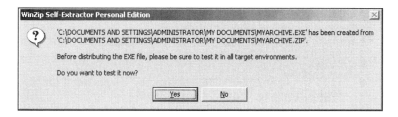

Figure 5-14: Creating a self-extracting archive

8. If you click No, you are returned to the main WinZip Self-Extractor
    Personal Edition screen. If you click Yes, the WinZip Self-Extractor screen
    appears as shown in Figure 5-15. This is the same screen that people will see
    when they open your self-extracting archive. Click Unzip to extract the
    archive, or change the default unzip location by entering a new folder name
    in the Unzip to folder field. (You can also click Run WinZip to unzip the
    archive using WinZip Classic, thereby bypassing the archive's self-extraction
    capabilities.)

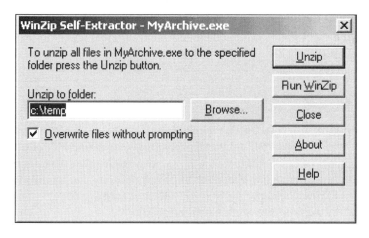

Figure 5-15: Testing your self-extracting archive

UUencoding a Zip File

The Internet is designed to transport information as text. Thus, Internet applications, such as email, convert data to text so that it can be transmitted over the
Internet. The recipient of the information then uses a similar application to
seamlessly convert the text back to its original format.

Not too many years ago, some email systems could not handle nontext files.
To help users stuck with these systems, WinZip includes a UUencode option
that allows you to convert Zip files into UUencoded text format. The recipient
of a UUencoded file can then use WinZip to extract its contents just as with any
other archive file.

To convert a Zip file to a UUencoded file, follow these steps:

1. Open the archive that you want to UUencode.
2. Select UUencode from the WinZip Actions menu.
3. Click OK. WinZip will tell you that the UUencoded file has been created, as shown in Figure 5-16.

Figure 5-16: UUencoding an archive

After you have UUencoded an archive, you should have two archives with the same name but with different file extensions. One will be your original archive with a .zip file extension, and the other will be the UUencoded file with a .uue file extension.

Verifying Archive Integrity

WinZip Test offers a quick way to test the integrity, or status, of your Zip file. This test makes sure that your file has not been corrupted in some way before you distribute your archive, and it does so without actually unzipping the archive.

Run WinZip Test by clicking the Test option on the Archive menu. When you run the program, a dialog box similar to the View Last Output screen in Figure 5-17 appears. The View Last Output utility checks the overall integrity of the Zip file and reports any errors. Then it tests the files within the Zip file to make sure that each can be properly unzipped.

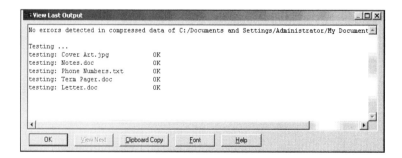

Figure 5-17: Verifying the integrity of your archive

Click OK to close this screen, or click Clipboard Copy to copy its output to the Windows clipboard so that you can paste it into a program like Notepad. (The Font button lets you change the appearance of the report.)

NOTE *Testing may take a while if you're running the test on a large archive. To cancel the test once it's begun, press ESC.*

Adding Comments to Archives

It is often useful to add instructions or documentation to your archives in a comment that appears as soon as the archive is opened. For example, if your archive contains family pictures that you are sending to a relative, you might include a short message describing them. Or if your archive contains confidential information, you might want to include a comment that reminds anyone who opens it that its contents are confidential.

There are two ways to add comments to a Zip file. One common though not WinZip-specific way to do so is to create a text file (for example, readme.txt) with the information that you want to display and then to add that file to the archive in the hope that people will read it—though often they will not. A better approach is to use WinZip's Comment feature to ensure that your information is displayed when people unzip your archive, as follows:

1. Open the Zip file to which you want to add the comment.
2. Select the Comment option on the Actions menu; the Comment screen appears, as shown in Figure 5-18.

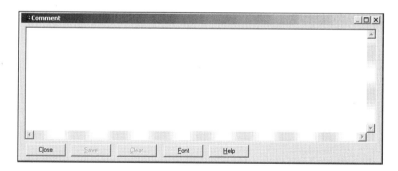

Figure 5-18: Adding a comment to your Zip file

3. Enter a comment. (Click Clear at any time to start over, or click Font to change the appearance of your text.)
4. Click Save when you're done.

NOTE *If you click Close before entering text, WinZip will not add a comment to the Zip file. But if you enter any text, even a blank space, WinZip will ask you whether to save the comment before closing the Comment screen.*

Once you have added your comment to your Zip file, it will appear automatically when the Zip file is opened, as shown in Figure 5-19.

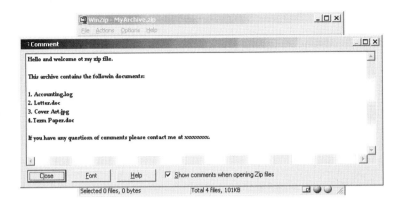

Figure 5-19: Comments appear automatically whenever the Zip file is opened

Checking Out Archive Programs and Files

The WinZip CheckOut feature enables you to work with the contents of an archive without extracting the contents. It does so by extracting the contents to a temporary folder, displaying the folder's contents, and allowing you to work with the files. If the temporary folder contains other files, WinZip prompts you for permission to delete them in order to ensure that only the contents of the archive are present.

To check out an archive, do the following:

1. Open the archive that you want to work with and then click the CheckOut option on the Actions menu. The CheckOut screen will appear, as shown in Figure 5-20.

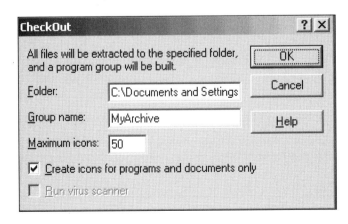

Figure 5-20: CheckOut lets you examine an archive's contents before permanently unzipping the files

2. In the Folder field, type the location of the temporary folder where the files will be opened; if the folder does not exist, WinZip will create it.

3. Specify any of the following options:

Group name. This field allows you to type a message that will appear in the title bar of the window that WinZip opens to display the archive's contents. For example, when checked out, the contents of the archive listed in Figure 5-20 will appear in a window whose title bar displays the group name message MyArchive, as shown in Figure 5-21.

Maximum icons. This setting lets you limit the number of icons that can be created in your checkout folder.

Create icons for programs and documents only. This option limits the creation of icons to just those two types of files.

Run virus scanner. If you have configured WinZip to work with a virus scanner, the Run virus scanner option will be enabled, allowing to you scan the contents of the archive. If a virus is found, the checkout process will terminate, and your antivirus program will warn you.

4. Click OK to run CheckOut. Figure 5-21 shows the window that WinZip opens to display the archive's files.

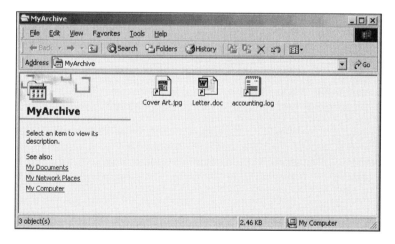

Figure 5-21: Viewing the files in the folder created by the checkout process

TIP   *If you close the checkout window before you are finished working with it, you can reopen it by clicking Start • Programs and then the group name that you assigned when you began the checkout process.*

5. When you close the archive or exit WinZip, WinZip will ask whether you want to delete the folder and files created by the checkout process. Click Yes to have WinZip remove the folder and its contents as well as the program group on the Start menu. Click No if you want WinZip to leave everything in place.

Automatically Installing Archive Programs

WinZip can automatically install a program in an archive if the archive contains a setup.exe file. It can also install screen savers or desktop themes contained in Zip files. To see this process in action, open an archive that contains one of these files and then click the Install option on the Actions menu. You should see the Install screen, shown in Figure 5-22.

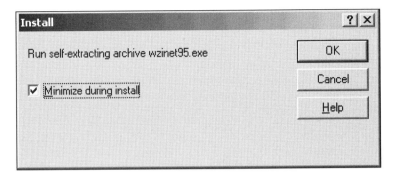

Figure 5-22: Installing software located in your Zip files

If you leave the Minimize during install option selected, WinZip will run minimized when the installation process executes. Click OK to begin the installation, or click Cancel to terminate the process. If you choose to complete the installation, WinZip will copy the contents of the Zip file to a temporary folder and then run the setup program. When the installation process is complete, WinZip will delete the temporary folder and its files.

6

WINZIP CLASSIC CONFIGURATION OPTIONS

This chapter shows you how to configure WinZip and its many features. You'll learn how to tailor WinZip to work the way you want it to so that you can be as efficient as possible. For example, you'll learn how to customize the WinZip toolbar so that the features you use most often are always just a single click away.

You'll also learn how to configure external applications such as your antivirus program to work with WinZip so that you can work safely and securely, and how to secure files in your archives with password protection. By the time you are done with this chapter, you will know a lot more about WinZip and the way that it works.

In Chapter 3, "The WinZip Wizard," you learned how to configure the WinZip Wizard. This chapter provides similar instruction on configuring WinZip Classic.

To begin configuring WinZip Classic, select one of the configuration options from the Options menu on WinZip's main screen. Each option lets you configure a specific aspect of WinZip. These are the options available:

Configuration. Provides access to most of WinZip's configuration options.

Password. Lets you secure an archive with a password. (This option is available only if you have an archive open.)

Sort. Lets you change the order in which files are displayed when viewing the archive's contents.

Reuse WinZip Windows. Determines whether or not you can run two copies of WinZip at the same time.

Save Settings on Exit. Tells WinZip to automatically save any unsaved configuration changes before closing.

Save Settings Now. Tells WinZip to save configuration changes as soon as they are made.

Set Installation Defaults. Restores WinZip's default configuration settings.

View Last Output. Displays a log showing the results of the last WinZip operation. This option is available only when you have an open archive and have performed at least one operation on it such as adding a new file.

The Configuration Screen

Most of WinZip Classic's configuration options are located on the Configuration screen, where everything is organized on six tabs, or property sheets:

View. Provides options for controlling WinZip Classic's appearance, including which columns will be shown.

Toolbar. Allows you to customize the WinZip toolbar.

Folders. Specifies the locations of default WinZip folders, including the Startup, Extract, and Add folders.

System. Configures the way WinZip and Windows work together.

Program Locations. Allows you to configure other programs to work with WinZip, such as your virus scanner.

Miscellaneous. Contains configuration options that do not fall into the other categories.

Controlling WinZip's Appearance with View

The View property sheet is divided into three sections, as shown in Figure 6-1. The Columns section allows you to specify the columns of information that are displayed in the WinZip Classic main display area, including Type, Modified, Size, and so on. As Figure 6-1 shows, not every column is displayed by default (Type, CRC, and Attributes are unchecked) because WinZip displays only those columns that are likely most important for you to see. Check or uncheck any column to add or clear its selection, or click the Defaults button to restore WinZip to its original column selections.

The General section provides the following three options, which configure how data is displayed and selected in the main WinZip display area:

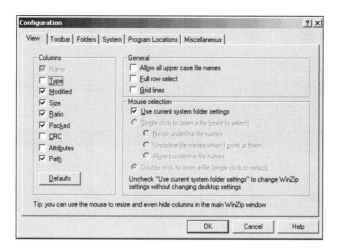

Figure 6-1: Configuring the WinZip Classic display

Allow all upper case file names. Tells WinZip to display file names without lower-case characters in all uppercase. Normally, WinZip capitalizes only the first letter of a file name.

Full row select. By default, you can select files only by clicking in the Name column. This option lets you select a file by clicking in any column in the WinZip display area. Turning this option on can make WinZip Classic easier to work with by widening the selection area from just the file name to the entire row.

Grid lines. Tells WinZip to overlay the display with a grid. Figure 6-2 shows how gridlines appear when configured for display. This option can make it easier to examine the contents of large archives by organizing their contents into a spreadsheet-like display.

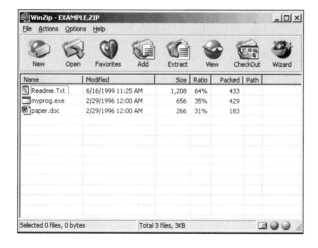

Figure 6-2: Use gridlines to format the display of an archive's contents

The Mouse selection section lets you configure the behavior of your mouse when working with WinZip. By default, WinZip uses the Windows mouse settings, but you can change the way WinZip interprets single and double mouse clicks by using these options.

Adding and Removing Toolbar Icons

The Toolbar property sheet's six configuration options control the appearance and behavior of the WinZip toolbar, as shown in Figure 6-3.

Use Explorer-style toolbar buttons. Replaces the default WinZip Classic toolbar with an Internet Explorer-style toolbar. This is the only Toolbar option that is disabled by default. You will probably find WinZip's default toolbar more attractive.

Use large toolbar buttons. Tells WinZip to use large buttons on the WinZip Classic toolbar. Disabling this option provides a little more room for the display of archive contents but otherwise provides no major benefit.

Show button text. Determines whether the name of the icon is displayed beneath its image; when this option is selected, labels are displayed.

Show tool tips. Determines whether WinZip displays small pop-up messages describing the function of buttons when you pass your cursor over them. Tooltips are handy when you forget what an icon does. Just move the pointer over a button, and WinZip will explain its function.

Use flat toolbar buttons. Replaces WinZip's 3D-style icons with two-dimensional icons. This option is designed to accommodate older computers with limited graphics capabilities.

Use high color toolbar buttons when possible. Determines the color range that WinZip is permitted to use when displaying icons. This option is enabled by default, and disabling it may make your display less attractive. (There's probably no need to uncheck either of the last two options unless you're using a really old machine with a really old monitor.)

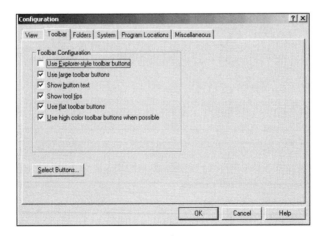

Figure 6-3: Configuring the WinZip Classic toolbar

Click the Select Buttons button at the bottom of the screen to add or remove icons on the WinZip Classic toolbar, as shown in Figure 6-4.

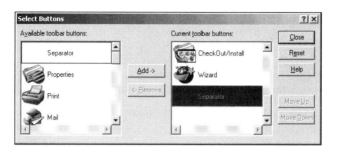

Figure 6-4: Adding or removing icons on the WinZip Classic toolbar

To add an icon to the toolbar, select it from the Available toolbar buttons list and click Add. To remove a toolbar icon, select it from the Current toolbar buttons list and click Remove. The list of icons on your toolbar will match the list in the Current toolbar buttons window.

To change the location of a toolbar icon, select it and click the Move Up or Move Down button. This moves the icon up or down in the list, which in turn determines where the icon appears on the WinZip toolbar. Click the Close button when you've finished making your changes, or click Reset to return your toolbar to WinZip's original configuration.

TIP *You can also configure the WinZip Classic toolbar right from the WinZip Classic screen. To do so, press and hold ALT and then drag a toolbar icon to a new location on the toolbar.*

Configuring Folder Options

The Folders property sheet lets you specify any of six default file locations used by various WinZip features, as shown in Figure 6-5.

Start-up folder. Sets the folder that WinZip uses when it opens or creates Zip files. You can choose System default (usually the WinZip folder), Last open archive (the folder used to open the last archive), or Folder (any folder that you specify).

Extract folder. Sets the folder that WinZip uses as the default folder for archive extractions. You can choose Open archive folder (the folder that contained the archive), Last extract folder (the last folder used to extract an archive), or Folder (any folder that you specify).

Add folder. Sets the folder that WinZip uses by default when adding files to an archive. You can choose Open archive folder (the folder that holds the archive), Last add folder (the last folder used by Add), or Folder (any folder that you specify).

Working folder. Sets the folder that WinZip uses by default when creating temporary Zip files. Temporary files are created by WinZip when performing an operation and are deleted once the operation is completed. Unless you specify a folder, WinZip will use the folder where the current archive resides. (Select the Use for

Removable media only option to restrict the use of this option to removable disks, such as floppies.)

CheckOut base folder. Sets the folder that WinZip uses by default as the parent folder for CheckOut operations. WinZip copies the contents of an archive to this folder temporarily so that you can examine it. Once you have finished checking the files, WinZip deletes the temporary files. If you do not specify a folder, WinZip uses the folder that contains the archive. More information about the checkout operation is available in Chapter 5, "Working with the Files in Your Archives."

Temp folder. Sets the folder that WinZip uses by default when creating temporary files. WinZip creates temporary files for a number of WinZip operations, such as virus scanning. For example, when you run a virus scan, WinZip extracts the files in an archive to this folder, runs your antivirus scanner on them, and then deletes them from the folder.

NOTE *By default, WinZip uses the same folder as both its working folder and temporary folder. There really is no need to change this because these two folders are essentially the same thing. However, for some operations involving floppy disks, WinZip will try to store temporary folders on the floppy disks, which can cause problems if the floppy runs out of space. Using the Working folder Use for removable media only option lets you to tell WinZip where to place temporary files to avoid running out of space on a floppy disk.*

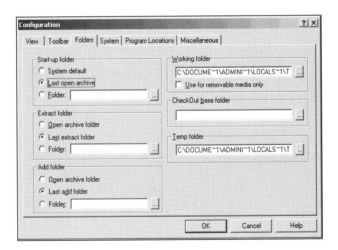

Figure 6-5: Configuring WinZip folders

Configuring System Settings

The System property sheet, displayed in Figure 6-6, is divided into three sections: General, Show Add dialog when dropping files on, and Explorer Shell Extension. The General section allows you to control the types of archive files WinZip works with and where shortcuts to WinZip are placed.

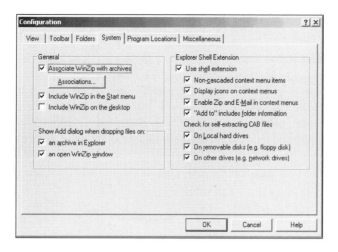

Figure 6-6: Configuring WinZip system settings

Associate WinZip with archives. Configures Windows to use WinZip as the default application for working with archives. The Associations button opens the WinZip Associations screen, shown in Figure 6-7. By default all listed archive types are selected. Clearing an archive's selection removes WinZip as the registered Windows application associated with that archive file type, but unless you have a specific reason to do so, you should not remove any of these associations.

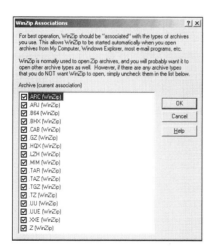

Figure 6-7: Managing WinZip associations with different archives

Include WinZip in the Start menu. Adds an entry for WinZip on the Windows Start menu.

Include WinZip on the desktop. Places a WinZip shortcut on the Windows desktop.

The section Show Add dialog when dropping files on offers two options for controlling what WinZip does when you drag and drop a file on an archive:

An archive in Explorer. Determines whether the Add dialog box appears when you drop a file on an archive in Windows Explorer or the Windows desktop. If this option is checked, the Add screen appears. For example, if you drop a file on a Zip file's icon and this option is enabled, the WinZip Add screen appears. You can then configure any of WinZip Add screen's options as discussed in Chapter 4 and click Add to add the file to the Zip file.

An open WinZip window. Determines whether the Add dialog box appears when you drop a file on an open WinZip window. If this box is checked, the Add screen appears.

The Explorer Shell Extension section provides several configuration options that affect the integration of WinZip features with Windows.

Use shell extension. Enables WinZip Explorer context menus and provides support for WinZip drag-and-drop operations. This option controls whether the other options in the Use shell extension section are enabled.

Non-cascaded context menu items. Allows WinZip to display submenu items on context menus. For example, right-click a file, and you will see a number of WinZip options on the file's context menu. If you disable this option, those options will disappear.

Display icons on context menus. Tells WinZip to add a small WinZip icon to each WinZip context menu. This option makes it easier to find Windows context menu options.

Enable Zip and E-mail in context menus. Determines whether the Zip and E-mail options appear in the context menu when you right-click a file.

"Add to" includes folder information. Tells WinZip to add folder information for files in the current folder as well as in subfolders when you add files to a Zip file by right-clicking it and selecting an Add to zip context menu option.

On local hard drives. Tells WinZip to check to see whether an .exe file is a self-extracting CAB file when displaying a context menu for a file on a local hard disk.

On removable disks (e.g., floppy disk). Tells WinZip to check to see whether an .exe file is a self-extracting CAB file when displaying a context menu for a file on a floppy disk.

On other drives (e.g., network drives). Tells WinZip to check to see whether an .exe file is a self-extracting CAB file when displaying a context menu for a file on a network disk.

Setting Up Connections to External Programs

Use the Program Locations property sheet, shown in Figure 6.8, to configure the way that WinZip interacts with a number of other programs. Although none of these programs is required for normal WinZip use, each extends WinZip's capabilities. These are the program associations available:

Viewer. Specifies the location of a viewer application, such as the Windows QuickView program, which lets you view certain files quickly without launching their original application.

Make .EXE. Sets the location of the program to be used to create self-extracting archives. The default setting is the location of WinZip Self-Extractor Personal Edition. For more information on creating self-extracting Zip files, see Chapter 5, "Working with the Files in Your Archives."

Scan program. Specifies the location of your antivirus program.

Parameters. Specifies parameters, or instructions passed to your antivirus program that tell it how you want it to run when WinZip asks it to scan the contents of an archive. WinZip will automatically configure this field if you are running one of WinZip's supported antivirus programs (discussed in Chapter 5, "Working with Archive Contents") when WinZip is installed. If you use an unsupported antivirus program, see its documentation to determine which options it requires to run from the command line. For example, the parameter %d can be used to pass the drive and folder of the files to be scanned. (See WinZip help for additional information on supported parameters.)

Run minimized. Prevents your virus scanner's screen from appearing when running a virus scan. If you disable this option, your antivirus program will open when WinZip runs, and you will have to close it manually once it completes its scan. This option works with the Parameters option.

ARJ. Sets the location of the ARJ program, an optional, third-party compression program that allows WinZip to manage .arj archives.

LHA. Sets the location of the LHA program, an optional, third-party compression program that allows WinZip to manage .lha archives.

ARC. Sets the location of the ARC program, an optional, third-party compression program that allows WinZip to manage .arc archives.

For more information on ARJ, LHA, and ARC archives, see Chapter 1, "WinZip Basics."

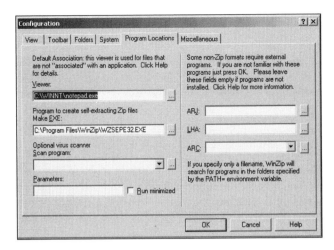

Figure 6-8: Configuring support for external programs

Miscellaneous WinZip Configuration Settings

The Miscellaneous property sheet contains two collections of settings, as shown in Figure 6-9. The first collection, in the Start-up section, includes these options:

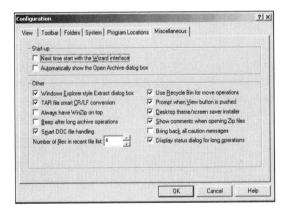

Figure 6-9: Setting miscellaneous WinZip configuration options

Next time start with the Wizard interface. Tells WinZip to load the WinZip Wizard when WinZip starts.

Automatically show the Open Archive dialog box. Tells WinZip to automatically open the Open Archive screen when WinZip starts.

The second collection of settings, displayed under the heading Other, covers a wide range of WinZip options.

Windows Explorer-style Extract dialog box. Tells WinZip to use a Windows Explorer-style interface. When this option is unchecked, WinZip displays files and folders using a Windows 3.1 File Manager-style view. Use this option if you prefer the look and feel of the old-style Windows 3.1 File Manager.

TAR file smart CR/LF conversion. Tells WinZip to translate TAR files so that character return and line-feed codes are properly interpreted. A TAR file is a type of archive used on UNIX systems. If you work with TAR files and leave this option disabled, some TAR files will be displayed as a continuous line of text. Turning this option on restores character return and line-feed codes so that the file is displayed as originally formatted.

Always have WinZip on top. Prevents other applications from sitting on top of WinZip on your screen.

Beep after long archive operations. Tells WinZip to beep when completing any operation that takes more than 1 second to complete. This option comes in handy when you have a very large archive, say 100MB, and want to work with another application while WinZip unzips it. You'll know WinZip is done when you hear the beep.

Smart DOC file handling. Tells WinZip to open all ASCII text files with a .doc file extension using its built-in viewer. If this option is not selected, WinZip will open the file in the associated application.

Number of files in recent file list. Displays a value between 0 and 9 specifying the number of recent archives WinZip keeps in its recently used files list on the File menu.

Use Recycle Bin for move operations. Tells WinZip to place a copy of any moved archive in the Windows Recycle Bin.

Prompt when View button is pushed. Tells WinZip to display a list of viewers when the View button in WinZip Classic is clicked. For more information on working with the View options, see Chapter 5, "Working with the Files in Your Archives."

Desktop theme/screen saver installer. Enables WinZip's theme and screen saver installer, which gives WinZip the ability to install any Windows theme or screen saver found in Zip files.

Show comments when opening Zip files. Tells WinZip to automatically display comments, if present, when opening a Zip file. Sometimes the creator of a Zip file may have some information to share regarding a Zip file such as a description of its contents or contact information. Leaving this option enabled allows WinZip to display comments when present whenever you open a Zip file. For more information on comments, see Chapter 5, "Working with the Files in Your Archives."

Bring back all caution messages. Tells WinZip to reenable any WinZip caution messages that you have disabled. Caution dialog boxes include any screen that contains a Do not display this dialog in the future option, such as the dialog box that appears when you start WinZip using the WinZip Wizard and then close it using WinZip Classic.

Display status dialog for long operations. Tells WinZip to display a progress indicator screen during lengthy operations. This screen resembles the dialog boxes that you see when copying or moving Windows files and will automatically disappear when the WinZip operation completes.

Password Protecting Archives

To protect individual files in an archive, you can password protect them. When you do, the file will be encrypted so that people with access to your archive will still be able to view its contents, but they will be prompted for the password when trying to open a password-protected file. WinZip identifies password-protected files with a + sign at the end of the file's name.

NOTE *You can password protect files only as you add them to a Zip files. To password protect a file already in an archive, extract the file and then add it back to the archive with password protection.*

To password protect archive files, follow these steps:

1. Open an archive; then click the Password option on the Options menu. The Password screen appears as shown in Figure 6-10.

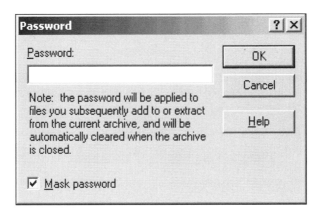

Figure 6-10: Protecting archive files with a password

2. Type your password and make sure that the Mask password option is selected so that no one can see your password as you type it. Click OK

3. When prompted, retype the password.

4. Now add the new file to the archive. Each file that you add will be encrypted.

NOTE *If you close a password-protected archive and then reopen it to add more files, those files will not be encrypted unless you repeat the password-protection procedure.*

Sorting Archive Contents

To configure the way that files are displayed in the main WinZip Classic display area, specify a sort order. To sort based on any column heading, select the Sort option on the Options menu and then select a column name, as shown in Figure 6-11.

Figure 6-11: Specifying the default sort order

You can sort on any column regardless of whether it is displayed.

Running More Than One Copy of WinZip

You can set up WinZip so that it will allow you to run only one copy at a time or as many copies as you want. Choose between these options by selecting or clearing the Reuse WinZip Windows option on the Options menu, as shown in Figure 6-12. When this option is selected, you can open multiple copies of WinZip simultaneously.

Figure 6-12: Determining whether to permit multiple instances of WinZip

Viewing the Previous WinZip Operation

The last entry on the WinZip Options menu is the View Last Output option (dimmed in Figure 6-14), which gives access to a description of the results of the most recently run WinZip command, as shown on the View Last Output screen in Figure 6-13.

Figure 6-13: Reviewing the results of your last WinZip command

For example, Figure 6-13 shows that the last action WinZip performed was a delete operation. In this example, a file stored in an archive was removed. The first two lines show that the user chose to include any system or hidden files when executing the Delete command. However, as the third line shows, only one file, accounting.log, was actually deleted. The last line shows that the archive was then saved (or replaced).

Saving Configuration Settings

WinZip give you two options for saving configuration changes: Save Settings on Exit and Save Settings Now. The first option waits until you close WinZip to save the changes, and the second saves them immediately. WinZip also makes it easy for you to restore all configuration options to their original settings with the Set Installation Default option. All three of these options are located on the WinZip Classic Options menu, as shown in Figure 6-14.

Figure 6-14: Managing WinZip configuration

7

WINZIP HELP

This chapter shows you how to get help with WinZip. You'll learn how to use WinZip's built-in tutorials and where to find answers to frequently asked questions (FAQs). You'll also learn how to work with WinZip help and where to find additional help at WinZip's website. You'll also find out how to purchase a licensed copy of WinZip and where to find a copy of the WinZip license agreement.

Introducing WinZip Help

WinZip comes with a complete and detailed help system, which you can reach by clicking the WinZip Help menu, as shown in Figure 7-1. From the Help menu, you can access all available WinZip documentation and connect to up-to-the-minute help on the WinZip website.

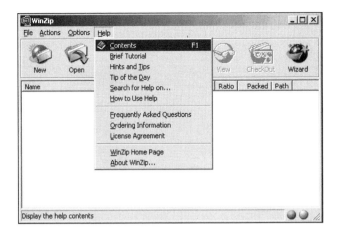

Figure 7-1: Viewing WinZip help

Help Options

The first option on the WinZip Help menu, Contents, opens the Help Topics screen, with three different ways to search for help, as shown in Figure 7-2. The three methods for searching for WinZip help, Contents, Index, and Find, all have access to the same information—they just handle it differently.

Figure 7-2: Viewing WinZip's documentation

The Contents tab is like a table of contents for WinZip help. The Index tab gives you access to a comprehensive index of WinZip information that you can quickly navigate by typing a few letters of the topic that you are interested in. For example, Figure 7-3 shows the results of an index search for information on the WinZip Comment feature.

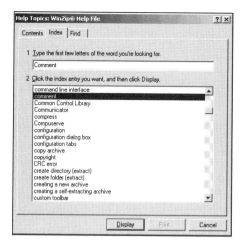

Figure 7-3: Searching WinZip's help index

If you can't find what you're looking for on either the Contents or Index tab, try a more thorough search with the Find tab. For example, Figure 7-4 shows the results of searching with Find for the term *self-extracting*.

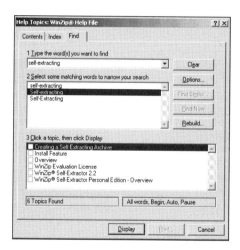

Figure 7-4: Finding a help topic

WinZip displays its help information in a straightforward manner, as shown in Figure 7-5.

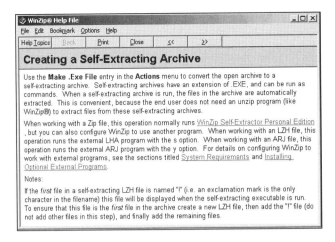

Figure 7-5: Viewing a typical WinZip help topic

The six navigation buttons at the top of the screen (Help, Back, Print, Close, and << and >>) help you work with the help system. Click Help to return to the three tabs that make up the WinZip help system. Back takes you to the previously viewed help page, Print lets you print the current topic, Close closes the help system, and the << and >> buttons take you forward and backward through the available help. WinZip's help text includes links to related help topics, which may even include Internet-based content.

The Built-in WinZip Tutorials

Two WinZip help features that you may want to examine are the ten lessons in the WinZip Tutorial and the WinZip tutor. Access the tutorial by choosing Help • Brief Tutorial on the WinZip Help menu, as shown in Figure 7-6.

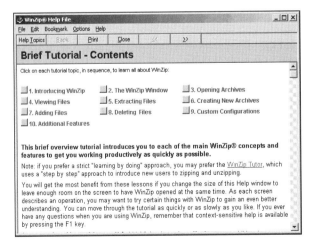

Figure 7-6: Using the WinZip tutorial

You can also click the WinZip Tutor link on the Brief Tutorial – Contents page to access the WinZip Tutor, shown in Figure 7-7. The WinZip tutor shows you, interactively, how to zip and unzip files with WinZip Classic.

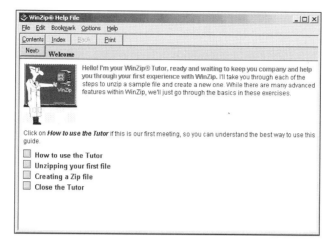

Figure 7-7: WinZip Tutor

WinZip Hints and Tips

Another rich source of information about WinZip is its collection of hints and tips for using WinZip, shown in Figure 7-8. You can access this information by selecting the Hints and Tips option on the WinZip Help menu.

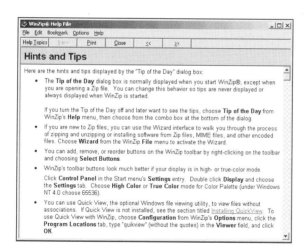

Figure 7-8: WinZip Hints and Tips

Viewing the Tip of the Day

The WinZip Tip of the Day, shown in Figure 7-9, is automatically displayed each time WinZip starts and is designed to provide you with a helpful tip about using WinZip. To turn off this option, choose Help • Tip of the Day and then choose Never show tips at startup from the drop-down list in the lower-left corner of the display. To turn the display back on, choose Show tips at startup if not opening an archive.

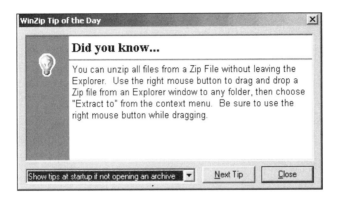

Figure 7-9: The WinZip Tip of the Day

Frequently Asked Questions

WinZip includes links to two collections of frequently asked questions, or FAQs. To browse these collections, choose Help • Frequently Asked Questions on the WinZip Help menu. This opens the Frequently Asked Questions screen shown in Figure 7-10.

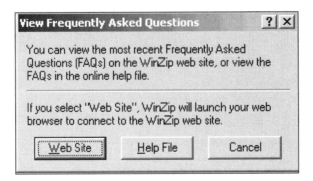

Figure 7-10: Choosing between WinZip local and online FAQs

You will find that the local and the online FAQs contain a lot of the same information. The local copy will be faster to access, while the online copy will always be the more current of the two. Click the Help File button on the Frequently Asked Question screen to view the local copy of WinZip FAQs. It looks like any other WinZip help topic, as shown in Figure 7-11.

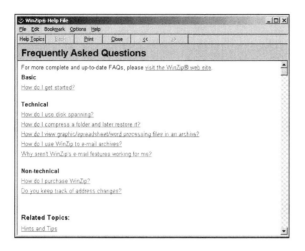

Figure 7-11: Viewing WinZip's local FAQs

WinZip's FAQs are organized into three categories:

Basic. Answers questions about how to get started with WinZip.

Technical. Answers more advanced questions about using WinZip, such as how to perform disk spanning.

Non-technical. Answers nontechnical questions about such topics as how to purchase WinZip.

You can view the Internet collection of WinZip FAQs, as shown in Figure 7-12, by clicking the Web Site button on the Frequently Asked Questions screen. The FAQs at the WinZip website will always be the most current ones, although in most cases you will find the same information in your local copy of WinZip's FAQs. One particularly nice feature of the web-based FAQs page, though, is a search page that lets you search the entire WinZip website for answers.

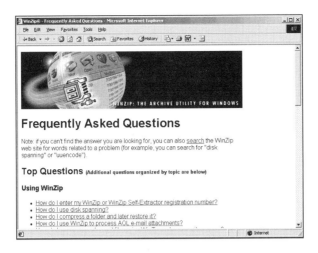

Figure 7-12: Viewing the WinZip FAQs online

8

OPERATING SYSTEM INTEGRATION

WHAT YOU'LL LEARN
In this chapter, you will:

- Create Zip files from the Windows desktop

- Use drag and drop to open, add, modify, and extract archive contents

- Take advantage of WinZip context menu options

- Print a file in an archive without opening it

As with most Windows applications, when you install WinZip, it adds itself to the Windows Start menu, places a shortcut for itself on the Windows desktop, and registers .zip as a WinZip file association. Windows maintains a list of applications and their associated file extensions. By registering the .zip file extension, WinZip tells Windows to automatically load any .zip files into WinZip when you double-click them. With these modifications to Windows, WinZip makes it easy for you to locate and start it and to open Zip files automatically with it.

But WinZip isn't satisfied with just making it easy for you to run WinZip. It also adds WinZip options to Windows context menus. Context menus are the menus you see when you right-click a Windows file or folder. For example, if you right-click any Windows file after installing WinZip, you'll see new WinZip options that allow you to add the file to a Zip file or use WinZip's Zip and E-mail option.

This chapter shows you how best to use WinZip's tight integration with Windows to work faster and more efficiently with your archives.

Locating WinZip and WinZip Components

When you installed WinZip, it created a folder named C:\Program Files\WinZip and installed all WinZip files inside it, as shown in Figure 8-1.

Figure 8-1: The contents of the WinZip folder

In addition to the Winzip32.exe file (which is the WinZip program itself), you'll find a number of useful files in this directory, most of which provide documentation or are help related. The files of note include the following:

Example.zip. A sample Zip file intended for use with WinZip help.

License.txt, Order.txt, Readme.txt, Vendor.txt, Whatsnew.txt, and WinZip.txt. Text files that supplement WinZip's online documentation. These text files provide information about the WinZip license agreement, how to purchase a copy of WinZip, how to install WinZip, and the rules for distributing WinZip, as well as a review of new features and miscellaneous information about WinZip.

Winzip.hlp, Wzinst.hlp, Wztutor.hlp, and Wzwizard.hlp. WinZip's help files. These files constitute WinZip's help system and include help on installing WinZip, WinZip Tutor help, and help for the WinZip Wizard.

Wzqkstrt.rtf. The WinZip Quick Start document; a mini-guide designed to help you begin using WinZip quickly.

Wzsepe32.exe. The WinZip Self-Extractor Personal Edition executable. This program provides WinZip's ability to create self-extracting Zip files, as discussed in Chapter 5, "Working with the Files in Your Archives."

WinZip File Associations

Windows uses file associations to identify which application to use to open files with a particular extension. For example, when you double-click an archived file with a .txt file extension while using WinZip Classic, WinZip will start the Windows' Notepad program and load the file in it.

In addition to registering the .zip file extension as a WinZip associated file extension, WinZip also registers a number of other archive file extensions, as listed in Chapter 6, "WinZip Classic Configuration Options." To view all registered Windows file extensions, including those registered by WinZip, from Windows Explorer, choose File • View • Options. When the Options screen appears, click the File Types tab to see a list of registered file extensions. Scroll down a bit, and you'll see an entry for WinZip, as shown in Figure 8-2.

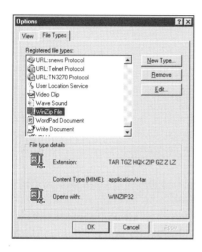

Figure 8-2: Viewing WinZip file associations

As Figure 8-2 shows, you can view some of WinZip's registered file associations from this screen, but not all. To view the rest, click Edit. A new screen appears showing all of WinZip's registered file extensions in the Default Extension for
Content Type drop-down list.

The current WinZip icon is displayed at the upper-left of the screen. Click Change icon. The Change Icon screen appears, as shown in Figure 8-3.

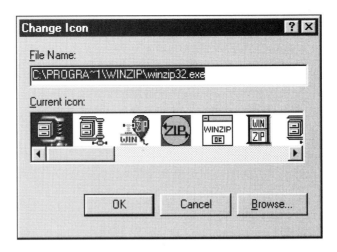

Figure 8-3: The Change Icon screen

WinZip's Windows Integration

During installation, WinZip integrates itself with Windows in many ways that make it look and act like a built-in Windows component. As you will see throughout this chapter, this means that you have access to much of WinZip's functionality from many places besides the Windows Start menu. This tight integration lets you do the following:

• Create new Zip files directly from the Windows desktop.

• Use Windows drag-and-drop functionality.

• Add WinZip context menu options to every Windows file and folder.

• Work with archives without opening WinZip.

• Right-click an archive and select Open with WinZip.

TIP *As you may know, Microsoft Windows keeps a list of files that you have recently used, which you can access by choosing Start • Documents as shown in Figure 8-4. If you've recently opened an archive and it appears in this list, you can click its shortcut to start a new WinZip session to work with the archive again.*

Figure 8-4: Opening a recently accessed archive in the Documents folder

Drag and Drop

One of the most useful Windows features integrated into WinZip is drag and drop, which allows you to click and hold your mouse over a file and then drag and drop it onto another file, a folder, or an application, such as WinZip.

For instance, you can drag and drop a file displayed in an archive being viewed with WinZip Classic right onto another open application, the application's icon, or a shortcut to the application. When you do, WinZip extracts the archive behind the scenes into a temporary folder and loads the file into the application. WinZip then waits for you to finish working with the file; then it deletes the temporary file.

For example, if you open a Zip file that contains multiple Microsoft Word documents, you can select as many of them as you want and then drag and drop them onto a Microsoft Word shortcut, and Word will automatically start and load each file individually. A variation of this technique allows you to drag and drop multiple Word files onto an open Word document, in which case each file is opened and appended to the end of the existing Word document.

As you learned in Chapter 4, "Managing Your Archives," WinZip also integrates with most Windows email applications, such as Outlook Express, using the Zip and Mail feature. In addition, you can use drag and drop to add one or more Zip files as attachments in most email applications.

You can use drag and drop with WinZip to do the following:

• Open any archive.

• Add files to an archive.

• Extract files from an archive.

• Move an archive from one location to another.

• Print an archive file.

• Open a file stored in an archive with another application.

Modifying Zip Files from the Windows Desktop

WinZip offers a number of ways for you to add new files to a Zip file from the Windows desktop. For example, you can add a file to an archive by right-clicking it and selecting Add to Zip from the Windows context menu that appears, as shown in Figure 8-5.

Figure 8-5: Right-click any Windows file to see that WinZip has added new WinZip options

When you choose this option, the WinZip Add screen appears, as shown in Figure 8-6. Enter the name of the archive to which you want to add the file, select any options, and click Add. (If you specify a new archive name, WinZip will create a new Zip file.)

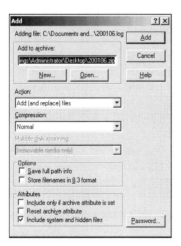

Figure 8-6: Adding files to a Zip file

TIP   *Press and hold the SHIFT or CTRL key while selecting files to add multiple files to an archive in a single step.*

You can also add files to an archive by dragging and dropping the file onto any of the following:

- An open Archive (using WinZip Classic)
- A Zip file's icon
- A shortcut to a Zip file

Normally, the WinZip Add screen appears when you drag and drop a file onto an archive. However, if you prefer, you can bypass this dialog box and have the file automatically added to the archive. To set up this option, open WinZip Classic, choose the Configuration menu, select the System property sheet, and clear the Show Add dialog when dropping files on an Archive in Explorer option.

To create a new Zip file and add files to it directly from the Windows desktop, right-click any open area on the desktop and select New • WinZip File from the pop-up menu, as shown in Figure 8-7.

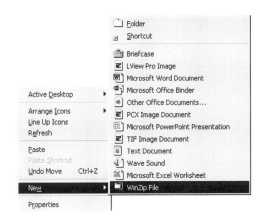

Figure 8-7: Creating a new Zip file from the Windows desktop

Unzipping Archives the Easy Way

One quick way to unzip an archive is to right-click its icon and select Extract to from the pop-up menu, as shown in Figure 8-8.

Figure 8-8: Extracting a Zip file without first loading it into WinZip

In response, WinZip will start and display the WinZip Classic Extract screen. Then all you need to do is choose where you want to unzip the archive and click Extract.

If you are using WinZip and already have an open archive, you can unzip some or all of its contents by selecting the files and dragging and dropping them onto the Windows desktop or any other Windows folder. Another drag-and-drop option for unzipping an archive is to right-click the file, drag it onto a Windows folder, and then release it. A pop-up menu will appear, as shown in Figure 8-9.

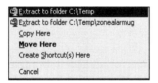

Figure 8-9: Extracting an archive by dropping it onto a folder

Two unzip options will be available:

Extract to folder x:\xxx. This option offers to unzip the archive in the folder where it was dropped. For example, if you drag and drop a file named Letter located inside an archive to a folder named MyFolder on your C: drive, this option will read Extract to folder C:\MyFolder. If you were to click this option, WinZip would extract the file and place it in C:\MyFolder.

Extract to folder x:\xxx\xxx. This option offers to create a new subfolder of the same name as the archive and to unzip the archive into it. For example, if you drag and drop a file named Letter located inside an archive to a folder named MyFolder on your C: drive, this option will read Extract to folder C:\MyFolder\ Letter. If you were to click this option, WinZip would first create a new subfolder named Letter inside C:\MyFolder and then extract the file and place it in C:\MyFolder\Letter.

Drag-and-Drop Printing

You can use drag and drop to print a file contained in an archive by opening WinZip Classic, selecting the file, and dragging and dropping the file onto a printer icon, as shown in Figure 8-10. WinZip will extract the file to a folder, send it to the printer, and then delete the temporarily extracted file.

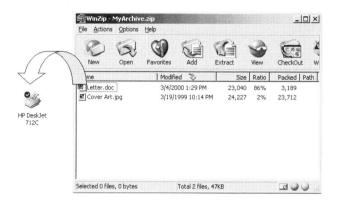

Figure 8-10: Using drag and drop to print an archive file

Miscellaneous Windows Integration Options

Just about every type of WinZip's Windows integration presented in this chapter is configured on the WinZip Configuration screen, discussed in Chapter 6, "WinZip Classic Configuration Options." For example, you can determine whether or not any WinZip options appear when you right-click a file or folder by enabling or disabling the Use shell extension option on the WinZip Configuration System property sheet, as shown in Figure 8-11. When enabled, this option allows you to configure a number of additional options, including these:

Non-cascaded context menu items. Displays all WinZip menu options when you right-click a Windows file or folder. When this option is disabled, a WinZip menu option labeled WinZip appears when you right-click a file or folder. Clicking this menu option displays a submenu where the WinZip options are displayed.

Display icons on context menus. Displays a small WinZip icon to the right of any menu option when you right-click a Windows file or folder.

Enable Zip and E-Mail in context menus. Determines whether you can use the WinZip Zip and E-mail feature. If this option is checked, it is enabled if WinZip detects a supported email system. When this option is disabled, the Zip and E-mail option is not displayed when you right-click a file or folder.

Add to includes folder information. Adds folder information to a Zip file when you add a new file by right-clicking it and selecting one of the Add to options discussed earlier in this chapter.

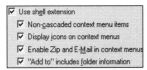

Figure 8-11: WinZip's shell extension options

Two other configuration settings that you may find helpful are located on the Configuration screen's Miscellaneous property sheet:

Always have WinZip on top. Prevents the WinZip Wizard or WinZip Classic interface from being overlaid by other Windows applications.

Use Recycle Bin for move operations. Places a copy of an archive in the Windows Recycle Bin whenever you move an archive to a different location.

9

BUILT-IN
COMMAND-LINE SUPPORT

WHAT YOU'LL LEARN
In this chapter, you will:

- Work with the Windows Run dialog box

- Work with the Windows command prompt

- Create Zip files from the command line

- Extract Zip files from the command line

The WinZip Wizard and WinZip Classic are not the only interfaces for working with WinZip. WinZip also includes a command-line interface for experienced WinZip users that allows you to work with Zip files from the Windows Run dialog box or from the Windows command line. The Windows Run dialog box, opened by choosing Start • Run, accepts typed commands and immediately executes them. The Windows command line, opened by choosing Start • Programs • Accessories • Command Prompt, also processes text commands. Although WinZip's built-in command line interface can zip and unzip Zip files, it cannot perform any of the other WinZip features that the WinZip Wizard and WinZip Classic provide.

Most users will not need to use WinZip's command-line interface. However, if you prefer working from the command prompt or are simply curious, you'll want to check out WinZip's built-in command-line support. Once you become proficient with the WinZip command-line interface, you'll find that it can save you time and a lot of mouse clicks when creating or extracting Zip files.

Running Commands from the Windows Run Dialog Box

Windows allows you to execute commands from its Run dialog box, shown in Figure 9-1. To open the Run dialog box, choose Start • Run; then enter your command in the Open field and click OK. Windows will then execute the command and close the dialog box.

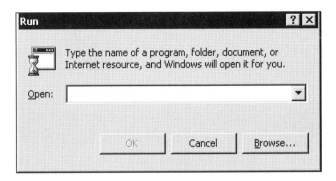

Figure 9-1: The Windows Run dialog box

For example, you can start WinZip from the Run dialog box by entering **winzip** and clicking OK.

The Run dialog box is great when you have only a single command to execute. However, if you want to run several commands, you should open a Windows command session and work from the command prompt, as discussed in the next section.

Working with the Windows Command Prompt

When most people think of Microsoft Windows, they usually think of using their mouse to point and click their way through the graphical user interface (GUI). The Windows GUI consists of the Windows desktop and the icons and other images that you see on your computer screen. However, each Windows operating system also offers access to a command-line interface known as the *command prompt*. The command prompt is a text-based interface that lets you interact with the operating system by entering Windows commands. Unlike the Windows Run command, the command prompt remains open after executing your commands, thus allowing you to view the results of your commands. Once the command prompt is open, you can enter Windows commands that perform many of the same tasks that you can perform from the Windows GUI.

To reach a command prompt in Windows 95 or 98, choose Start • Programs • MS-DOS Prompt. In Windows ME, choose Start • Programs • Accessories • MS-DOS prompt. In Windows NT 4 and 2000, choose Start • Programs • Accessories • Command Prompt.

For example, Figure 9-2 shows the Windows command prompt under Windows 2000 Professional. The C:\> is known as the Windows command prompt.

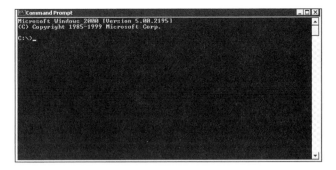

Figure 9-2: A Windows 2000 command session

The blinking underscore (_) character at the command prompt tells you where your typing will appear. When you type a command and press ENTER, Windows runs the command, displays its results, and then displays the command prompt again, telling you that it is ready for a new command.

When you have finished with the command prompt, close it by typing **exit** at the prompt and pressing ENTER.

Overview of WinZip's Command-Line Support

To start WinZip from the command prompt, follow these steps:

1. Open a command prompt.

2. Type **cd program files\winzip** and press ENTER to change to the WinZip folder.

3. Type **winzip32** and press ENTER to start WinZip.

As you will see in the next section, when you start WinZip from the command prompt, you can at the same time give it instructions for creating new Zip files or extracting the contents of existing ones.

Creating a New Archive from the Windows Command Line

To create a new Zip file from the command prompt, you enter a string of commands like the following:

```
WINZIP32 [-min] action [options] filename[.zip] files
```

WINZIP32 is the name of the WinZip program, and everything following it is an *argument*, an additional parameter that controls the way the command works. Command arguments inside brackets are optional, and italicized words (like *options* and *files*) are placeholders for arguments that you specify. For example, you would replace *files* with the name of a file that you want to add to a Zip file. Be sure to separate each part of the command with a space.

The -min argument tells WinZip to run minimized, unseen. You can leave this out with no problem; if you do, you will simply see WinZip open, run your command, and then close. If you do include the -min argument, it must come immediately after WINZIP32.

The *action* argument takes one of the following values:

-a   Tells WinZip to create a new Zip file.

-f   Tells WinZip to refresh an existing archive.

-u   Tells WinZip to update an existing archive.

-m   Tells WinZip to move the archive to a specified location.

You must specify one of the *action* arguments; each is the equivalent of an option in the Action section on the WinZip Classic Add screen, shown in Figure 9-3. (See Chapter 4, "Managing Your Archives," for more information on each option.)

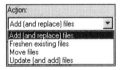

Figure 9-3: The action arguments are the same as those in the WinZip Classic Add screen's Action section

The *options* argument(s) are optional and can be any of a number of values, including these:

-r   Tells WinZip to add files and folders when adding files to the Zip file.

-p   Tells WinZip to include folder information for each file added to the Zip file.

You can specify one or both of these options, but if you specify both, be sure to separate them with a space. These two options are the same as those in the Folders section of the WinZip Classic Add screen, shown in Figure 9-4. (See Chapter 4, "Managing Your Archives," for more information on these options.)

Figure 9-4: The options arguments are the same as those in the WinZip Classic Add screen's Folders section

You can enter additional *options* arguments to specify the compression ratio to apply when creating a new archive:

-ex	Tells WinZip to create a Zip file using maximum compression.
-en	Tells WinZip to create a Zip file using normal compression.
-ef	Tells WinZip to create a Zip file using somewhat lower than normal compression.
-es	Tells WinZip to create a Zip file using its lowest compression.
-e0	Tells WinZip to create a Zip file without compression.

You can specify only one of these arguments at a time. If you don't include any of them, WinZip will use normal compression.

Each of these options is equivalent to an option in the Compression section of the WinZip Classic Add screen, shown in Figure 9-5. You can find more information on these options in Chapter 4, "Managing Your Archives."

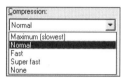

Figure 9-5: The compression arguments are the same as those in the WinZip Classic Add screen's Compression section

You can also specify an optional -hs argument that tells WinZip to include hidden and system files in a Zip file. Use the -hs argument when you want to make sure that you include every file in a folder, not just the visible ones. In addition, you can specify the optional -s*Password* option by replacing the *Password* portion of this argument with a password that will be used to encrypt each file added to the archive.

NOTE *The* Password *argument is case-sensitive, so you will need to supply both the correct spelling and case of the password when extracting the contents of the Zip file. Also, if the password contains a space, you must enclose it within quotation marks; for example, -s"My Password" would assign a password of My Password to each file added to an archive. Finally, if your password is longer than eight characters, you must place it in quotation marks regardless of whether it contains a space.*

Next, specify the *filename* argument; enter the file name you want to assign to the new Zip file, including the full path (drive and folder information). For example, to create an archive named MyArchive in the C:\temp folder you would enter **c:\temp\MyArchive**.

The final, required argument, *files*, specifies the file or files to be added to the Zip file. It can consist of any of the following combinations:

filename	Specifies the name of a file to be added to the Zip file.
filename with wildcards	Specifies the name of one or more files to add to the Zip file.
@filename	Specifies the location of a file that contains a list of files to be added to the Zip file.

*If you specify a file containing a list of files to add to an archive, each listed file must be on its own line. Be sure that the only item on each line is a file name, and that you do not include any extra blank spaces before or after the file name. In addition, each file must include a complete path, including drive, folder, and file name. For example, to include all files with a .doc extension in the Temp folder on the C drive, enter **C:\Temp*.doc** as the file name.*

There is nothing like a few good examples to help clarify the use of any command-line features. The following example demonstrates how to create a new Zip file named MyArchive in the Windows Temp folder, to contain all .doc files found in a folder named MyDocuments:

```
WINZIP32 -a c:\temp\MyArchive.zip c:\MyDocuments\*.doc
```

To test this command, do the following:

1. Open a Windows command session.
2. Type **cd program files\winzip** and press ENTER to change to the WinZip folder.
3. Type **WINZIP32 -a c:\temp\MyArchive.zip c:*.doc** and press ENTER to start WinZip.
4. WinZip will open, create the new Zip files, and then close. If you prefer not to see WinZip appear and then disappear, add the -min option to the command as shown here:

```
WINZIP32 -min -a c:\temp\MyArchive.zip c:\*.doc
```

The next example shows how to add all .txt files in the root directory to an existing Zip file, in this case c:\Temp\MyArchive. Here, we've added the password Secret so that each .txt file is encrypted when it is added to the archive.

```
WINZIP32 -min -u -sSecret c:\temp\MyArchive.zip c:\*.txt
```

The final example shows how to create a new archive that uses WinZip's highest compression ratio:

```
WINZIP32 -min -a -ex c:\temp\MyArchive.zip c:\*.doc
```

Extracting Archive Contents Using the Command Line

You can also use the WINZIP32.EXE command to extract the contents of a Zip file. When used to extract the contents of a Zip file, the WINZIP.32EXE command requires a different set of arguments than those used to create or modify an archive. The syntax for extracting the contents of a Zip file from the command line is:

```
WINZIP32 [-min] -e [options] filename[.zip] folder
```

WINZIP32 is the name of the WinZip executable program. As in the earlier examples, command arguments within brackets are optional, and italicized words are placeholders for arguments that you specify. All command elements are separated by spaces. As you learned in the section that showed you how to create a new archive using the Winzip32 command, the optional -min argument tells WinZip to run minimized and unseen. If you omit this parameter, you will see WinZip open, run your command, and close. When specified, the -min argument must be the first argument following the WINZIP32 executable command.

The -e argument is a required parameter that tells WinZip to perform an extraction.

Three optional *options* arguments are supported when extracting Zip files:

-o   Tells WinZip to overwrite any files in the destination folder that may have the same file names as those found in the archive.

-j   Tells WinZip to extract archive files by ignoring any path information that may exist in the archive. When this is not specified, WinZip will extract the files in the archive and re-create any subfolders that may have existed when the archive was created.

-sPassword Tells WinZip the password required to extract an encrypted file from a Zip file.

Filename.zip specifies the name and path of the Zip file to be extracted, and *Folder* tells WinZip where to extract the archive's contents. If the specified folder does not exist, WinZip will create it during the extraction operation.

The following command shows how to extract the contents of the MyArchive Zip files created earlier in this chapter. The example assumes that none of the files in the archive is encrypted. All files are extracted to the c:\Unzipped folder.

```
WINZIP32 -e c:\Temp\MyArchive.zip c:\Unzipped
```

In this example, the -e indicates that you want to perform an extraction. The c:\Temp\MyArchive.zip argument identifies the location of the archive that you want to extract, and c:\Unzipped points to the folder where you want the unzipped file to be copied.

The next example performs the same task, but this time runs it in the background by adding the -min argument so that you do not see WinZip as it stops and starts:

```
WINZIP32 -min -e c:\Temp\MyArchive.zip c:\Unzipped
```

The next example opens the same file but this time uses the -o option to tell WinZip to overwrite any files in the destination folder with those in the Zip file:

```
WINZIP32 -min -e -o c:\Temp\MyArchive.zip c:\Unzipped
```

This final example shows how to extract Zip files that contain files encrypted with the password Secret. As you can see, the command looks a lot like the previous example except that the -o option has been replaced with the -s option immediately followed by the password for the encrypted file.

```
WINZIP32 -min -e -sSecret c:\Temp\MyArchive.zip c:\Unzipped
```

What to Do When You Need Greater Command-Line Control

The WINZIP32.EXE executable provides the ability to zip, modify, and unzip Zip files, but it is lacking in a number of areas. The makers of WinZip provide the WinZip Command Line Support Add-on to provide the missing functionality. The add-on module actually consists of two executables: WZZIP.EXE and WZUNSIP.EXE. The two programs do exactly what their names imply, allowing you to zip and unzip files from the command line, but they also support several options that provide a much more robust solution than the WINZIP32.EXE executable. These additional features include the ability to do the following:

- List archive contents.
- Print a file.
- Test the integrity of a Zip file.
- Sort command output.
- Exclude files when unzipping an archive.
- Display a "Press any key to continue" message.
- Simulate an unzip operation without actually unzipping an archive.
- Add comments to a Zip file.
- Delete files from a Zip file.
- Span multiple disks.

The WinZip Command Line Support Add-on is distributed as a free download from WinZip. As of the writing of this book, it is provided only as a beta product, which means that you use it at your own risk because WinZip has not yet certified it for general release. Unless you are planning to incorporate WinZip functionality into Windows scripts, you will probably find that this add-on module gives you much more than you need.

To learn more about the WinZip Command Line Support Add-on, check out Chapter 12, "Command-Line Support Add-on."

10

WINZIP INTERNET BROWSER SUPPORT ADD-ON

WHAT YOU'LL LEARN
In this chapter, you will:

- Learn how the WinZip Internet Browser Support Add-on works
- Install and configure the add-on
- Use the add-on to save time and effort when downloading and extracting archives
- Uninstall the add-on

The WinZip Internet Browser Support Add-on is a free download that configures your Internet Explorer or Netscape Communicator Internet browser to work with WinZip, thus helping to automate the process of downloading and working with archives. Download the add-on from www.winzip.com, where you'll find versions for Windows 95 and higher as well as Windows 3.1. You'll also find different versions for current and past versions of WinZip. (See the WinZip website for additional requirements.)

Once installed, the add-on configures your browser to run WinZip whenever you download an archive. This chapter shows you how to install, configure, and work with this handy WinZip add-on.

Overview

Once installed, the WinZip Internet Browser Support Add-on sets things up so that your Internet browser will automatically run WinZip once you've finished downloading an archive. WinZip then moves the archive to a default download folder (which you can specify) and opens it. If you use the WinZip Wizard, you can click Next to begin extraction, or, if you use WinZip Classic, you'll see the archive's contents displayed.

The WinZip Internet Browser Support Add-on does not work with self-extracting Zip files (those with a .exe extension), because it configures your browser to run WinZip when you download a file with a .zip extension. There is no way around this problem.

Installing the WinZip Internet Browser Support Add-on

After you've downloaded the add-on, close any open programs, including WinZip, and click the add-on's .exe file to install the program. When asked whether to install the add-on in the same folder as WinZip, click Yes. The License Agreement and Warranty Disclaimer screen appear, telling you that the add-on is distributed "as-is." Click Yes to accept the license agreement before continuing with the installation. After installation is complete, you can configure the add-on.

Configuring Internet Browser Options

The WinZip Internet Browser Support Add-on is preconfigured, but you can modify its settings using its configuration dialog box. To do so, choose Start • Programs • WinZip • Internet Browser Support Configuration (see Figure 10-1).

Figure 10-1: Configuring the WinZip Internet Browser Support Add-on

Here are your configuration options:

Move Internet Downloads to c:\download. Tells WinZip to move the file from the folder where it was downloaded to the specified folder.

Open Downloads After Moving. Tells WinZip to automatically load the archive after downloading (and optionally moving it).

Change Download Folder. Lets you specify the destination for downloaded archives.

In addition, the Check Compatibility Info on Web Site button opens your web browser and loads a WinZip web page, shown in Figure 10-2, where you will find the most current information about this add-on, including a list of supported Internet browsers.

Figure 10-2: The WinZip Internet Browser Support Add-On web page

Downloading New Archives from the Internet

Once you install and configure the add-on, you're done. The next time you use your browser to download a Zip file, the add-on should start automatically. For example, if you use Internet Explorer and click an archive, you will see a screen similar to the one shown in Figure 10-3.

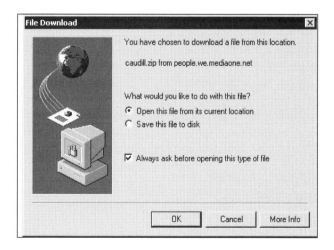

Figure 10-3: Select Open this file from its current location to run WinZip after downloading an archive

Select Open this file from its current location to tell Internet Explorer to run WinZip when the download completes. WinZip moves the archive according to your configuration settings. For example, if you use WinZip Classic, WinZip will run and display the contents of the archive as shown in Figure 10-4.

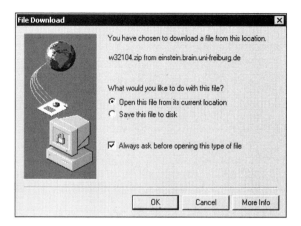

Figure 10-4: Your downloaded archive is automatically loaded into WinZip

Uninstalling the WinZip Internet Browser Support Add-on

To uninstall the browser add-on, choose Start • Settings • Control Panel, click the Add/Remove programs icon, and then remove the add-on from the list of installed applications to remove the program completely from your system.

NOTE *If you uninstall WinZip, both WinZip and the add-on will be removed.*

11

WINZIP
SELF-EXTRACTOR ADD-ON

WHAT YOU'LL LEARN
In this chapter, you will:

- Discover the advantages of using WinZip Self-Extractor

- Install WinZip Self-Extractor

- Create your own Self-extracting Zip files

The WinZip Self-Extractor Add-on is an optional WinZip component that brings advanced self-extraction capabilities to WinZip that go well beyond those of WinZip's built-in Self-Extractor Personal Edition utility. The add-on provides a wizard that steps you through the process of creating a self-extracting file from an existing Zip file. With this add-on, you'll be able to create self-extracting archives that span multiple disks, display custom messages, execute commands, and automatically run setup programs.

Introducing WinZip Self-Extractor

Unlike the WinZip Internet Browser Support Add-on and the Command-Line Support Add-on, the WinZip Self-Extractor Add-on must be purchased. However, as with WinZip, you may download and try it before deciding whether to buy it. Upgrades are free.

The WinZip Self-Extractor provides a number of features not found in the Self-Extractor Personal Edition that accompanies WinZip, including these:

- The ability to create a splash screen that appears when the self-extracting file is run.
- The ability to replace the default self-extractor icon.
- The ability to run a command after the extraction is complete.
- A wizard that steps you through the process of creating a self-extracting file.

You can use the WinZip Self-Extractor to create two different types of self-extracting archives:

Standard self-extracting files, which can be used to store regular Windows files.

Self-extracting files for software installation, designed to assist in the delivery and installation of software.

The primary difference between the two types of self-extracting Zip files is that the standard self-extracting file allows the user to overwrite the destination of the unzip folder and to decide whether to run an associated command. The software installation option, on the other hand, stores files in a temporary folder and then deletes the folder once the unzip operation is complete. If you specified a command to execute as part of the self-extracting Zip file, it is then executed.

Unless you write and develop your own software programs, you probably will use only the standard self-extraction file, so we'll focus on it in the rest of this chapter. You'll learn exactly how this option works in the section "Creating Your First Self-Extracting Zip File."

Installing the Add-on Module

Once you've downloaded the Self Extractor Add-on from www.winzip.com, double-click its .exe file to run it. You should see the WinZip Self-Extractor Setup dialog box, as shown in Figure 11-1. From here, follow these steps:

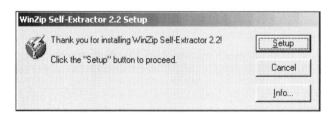

Figure 11-1: Getting ready to install the WinZip Self-Extractor

1. Click Setup.

2. You are asked to specify the installation folder for the add-on module. The default location is C:\Program Files\WinZip Self-Extractor. Either accept this location or enter a new one in the Install to field. Click OK.

3. The WinZip License Agreement and Warranty Display screen appears. Click View License Agreement to read its terms and then click OK to accept them.

4. The setup program displays a message asking if you would like to have WinZip's Make.Exe file menu automatically run the add-on module in place of the Self-Extractor Personal Edition, as shown in Figure 11-2. Click Yes.

NOTE *Until you purchase a license for your copy of the WinZip Self-Extractor Add-on, you will not be legally licensed to distribute any self-extracting Zip files that it creates. Therefore, you may want to leave the Self-Extraction Personal Edition as WinZip's default option until you purchase the add-on. When you are ready, you can rerun the install process and select the option to make the add-on the WinZip default.*

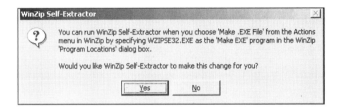

Figure 11-2: Configuring WinZip to automatically use the add-on

5. The installation process completes, and a prompt appears offering to run the WinZip Self-Extractor. Click Run WinZip Self-Extractor to begin working with the program, or click Done.

Introducing the WinZip Self-Extractor Add-on

To run the WinZip Self-Extractor, choose Start • Programs • WinZip Self-Extractor. The first time you run the add-on, you'll see a screen reminding you that you're using an unregistered copy and that, until you purchase a license, any self-extracting files you create are not legally licensed for distribution. Click OK to dismiss this screen; the Main WinZip Self-Extractor screen appears, as shown in Figure 11-3.

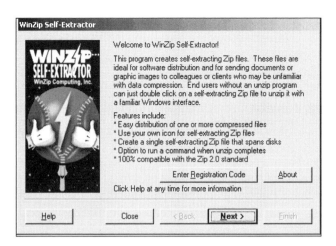

Figure 11-3: The WinZip Self-Extractor Add-on runs as a wizard that guides you through every step

You'll find the following options on the initial WinZip Self-Extractor screen:

Enter Registration Code. Allows you to register your copy of the add-on.

About. Provides version information.

Help. Opens the WinZip Self-Extractor help system.

Close. Closes the wizard.

Back. Allows you to go back and make changes to previous screens.

Next. Allows you to continue specifying options.

Finish. Allows you to create the self-extracting Zip file with the options you specified. The Self-Extractor will use defaults for any unspecified option(s).

NOTE *To uninstall the WinZip Self-Extractor, choose Start • Programs • WinZip Self-Extractor • Uninstall WinZip Self-Extractor.*

Registering Your Copy of the WinZip Self-Extractor

Once you purchase a license for the WinZip Self-Extractor, you will be assigned a registration code. To apply this code, start the WinZip Self-Extractor and click Enter Registration Code. The registration screen appears, as shown in Figure 11-4.

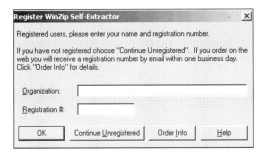

Figure 11-4: Registering your copy of the WinZip Self-Extractor Add-on

In the Organization field, enter the name you used when purchasing your license, and enter your registration code in the Registration # field; then click OK.

Creating Your First Self-Extracting Zip File

The WinZip Self-Extractor's sole purpose is to assist you in the creation of self-extracting Zip files. Here's how to do so:

1. Start the WinZip Self-Extractor.
2. The initial screen appears. Click Next.
3. Choose Standard self-extracting Zip file, as shown in Figure 11-5; then click Next.

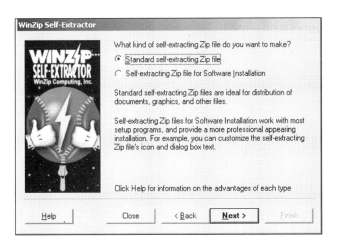

Figure 11-5: Creating a standard self-extracting Zip file

4. You are asked whether you want to create an archive that spans multiple removable disks, as shown in Figure 11-5. Unless you plan to store the archive on floppy disks, leave this option blank and click Next.

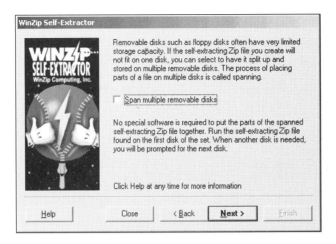

Figure 11-6: Self-extracting Zip files can also span multiple disks

5. Enter the name of the Zip file you want to make self-extracting, as shown in Figure 11-7; then click Next.

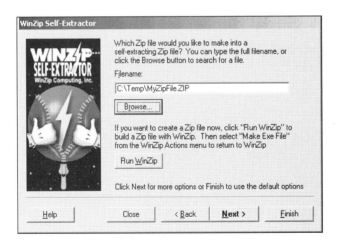

Figure 11-7: Any Zip file can be used to create a self-extracting Zip

NOTE *At this point, you have supplied the wizard with enough information to create a self-extracting file. If you click Finish, the archive will be created using default options in the same folder as the original Zip file. Or you may continue, configuring options as the wizard presents them until each has been configured. (Every screen from this point on includes a Finish button allowing you to stop at any point to create your self-extracting archive.)*

6. The next screen lets you create a splash screen that will be displayed when the self-extracting file is run, as shown in Figure 11-8. Enter a message in the entry box or specify the name and location of a text file that contains the message you want to appear. (The message can be up to 512 characters long.)

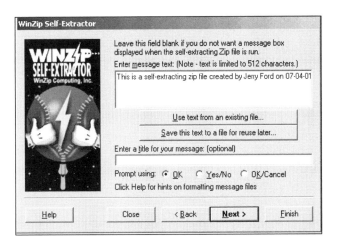

Figure 11-8: Adding a splash screen to a self-extracting Zip file

7. Enter a message that will appear in the title bar of the screen the user will see when running the archive, as well as decide which buttons will appear on the screen, including OK, Yes/No, and OK/Cancel. Make your selections and click Next.

8. On the next screen, as shown in Figure 11-9, you specify an Unzip to folder. If you leave this field blank, WinZip will use the Windows Temp folder. Click Next.

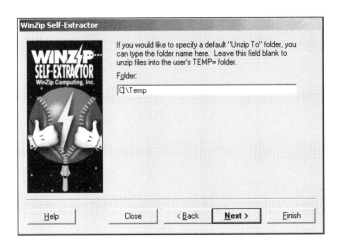

Figure 11-9: By default, the Windows Temp folder will be used to unzip the archive

9. On the next screen, enter a command you want to see run once the self-extracting file has finished running, as shown in Figure 11-10. Click Next.

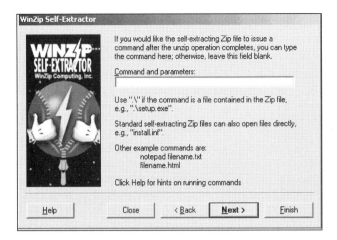

Figure 11-10: Adding a command to a self-extracting Zip file

10. On the next screen, as shown in Figure 11-11, you can add an About dialog box (up to 256 characters) that the user will see when running the file. You also specify the name and location of a text file that contains a message. Click Next.

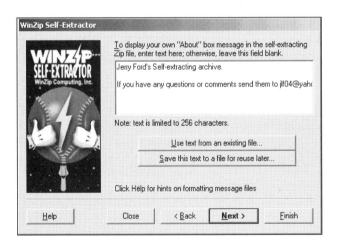

Figure 11-11: Adding an About dialog

11. Next you can specify the path and file name of an icon you want to use for the self-extracting file, as shown in Figure 11-12. If you don't specify one, the WinZip Self-Extractor icon will be used. Click Next.

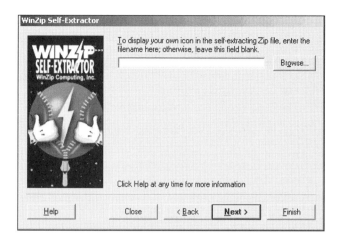

Figure 11-12: Adding a custom icon to the self-extracting Zip file

12. On the next screen, shown in Figure 11-13, choose from the following options:

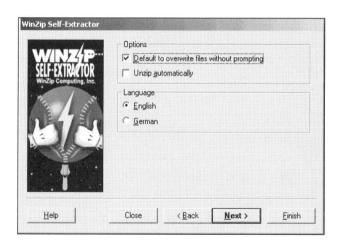

Figure 11-13: Completing the self-extracting Zip file

Default to overwrite file without prompting. Determines whether the user may decide whether duplicate files should be overwritten.

Unzip automatically. Sets the self-extracting archive to run automatically when its download completes.

English. Creates the file in English.

German. Creates the file in German.

13. A summary screen appears displaying your selected options. Use the Back button to go back and make any changes, or click Finish to create the self-extracting file.

14. If you click Next, you will see a screen stating that the file has been created. The Test self-extracting Zip file now option is selected by default. You can leave this option selected and click Next to test your self-extracting Zip file.

15. The last screen that you will see asks if you want to create another self-extracting file. Click Yes, take me through the wizard again to create another file, or click No, I am finished to close the wizard.

NOTE *If you had selected the disk-spanning option, you would have been prompted to supply as many floppy disks as necessary to create the self-extracting file. If you did not select this option, the file will be created in the same folder as the original Zip file. The new file will have the same file name as the original but will be slightly larger and have an .exe file extension.*

Running Your Self-Extracting Zip File

Self-extracting files have an .exe file extension and are run like any other Windows executable program. For example, when you double-click a standard self-extracting Zip file, it begins to run, and the screen shown in Figure 11-14 appears.

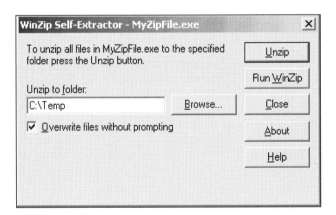

Figure 11-14: Running a standard self-extracting Zip file

The following options are displayed:

Unzip. Click to begin the extraction.

Run WinZip. Click to load the file into WinZip.

Close. Click to close the screen without unzipping the archive.

About. Click to read the About screen.

Help. Click to get help with this file.

Unzip to folder. Specify the folder where the archive should unzip its contents.

Overwrite files without prompting. Specify whether to be prompted when duplicates files exist in the destination folder.

NOTE *If you created a self-extracting Zip file for a software installation, the user will not see the same screen that is displayed when running a standard self-extracting file. Instead, a screen appears displaying just three options: Setup, Cancel, and About. The user can then click Setup to begin the extraction process, which will run as you configured it.*

12

COMMAND-LINE
SUPPORT ADD-ON

WHAT YOU'LL LEARN
In this chapter, you will:

- Install the add-on
- Use the add-on to unzip and zip files
- Create a simple script that works with WinZip

If you found WinZip's built-in command-line support useful, consider trying the WinZip Command-Line Support Add-on. Unlike WinZip's built-in support, which is limited to basic zipping and unzipping, the add-on provides access to most of WinZip's features, including the ability to test the integrity of Zip files, list Zip file contents, sort command output, span multiple disks, add comments, and delete files from archives.

Overview

The WinZip Command-Line Support Add-on is an optional application that provides advanced command-line capabilities. Unlike WinZip's built-in command-line support, this add-on exposes all of WinZip's functionality, meaning that you can perform just about any WinZip function without ever looking at the WinZip Classic or WinZip Wizard interface.

Installing the Command-Line Support Add-on

To install the add-on, download it from www.winzip.com and read its installation requirements and instructions there.

Once the add-on is installed, you should have the following links in the WinZip shortcut on Windows' Start menu:

* Command-Line Support Add-on Documentation
* Uninstall Command-Line Support Add-on

The add-on's command-line support comes in the form of two new commands:

* **WZZIP.EXE**. Used to create or update Zip files.
* **WZUNZIP.EXE**. Used to extract archives.

As with WinZip's built-in command-line support, you can execute these commands from the Windows command prompt, Run dialog box, or scripts. For information on working with the first two options, see Chapter 9, "Built-in Command-Line Support." You'll see an example of how to write a simple Windows script later in this chapter.

Using the WZZIP.exe Command

Use the WZZIP command to create new Zip files and to perform an assortment of other related options.

Following are some examples that should help you make sense of how to use this command. Detailed syntactical information on the WZZIP command is available in Appendix B, "WinZip Command-Line Support Add-on Reference."

The first example shows how to execute the WZZIP command in its simplest form. In this case, the only argument passed to the WZZIP command is the name of the Zip file to create. By default, all files in the current folder will be added to a Zip file named Myarchive.zip.

```
wzzip Myarchive.zip
```

Similarly, the following example adds all .log files in the c:\temp folder to a Zip file called Myarchive.zip:

```
wzzip Myarchive.zip c:\temp\*.log
```

The following example lists the contents of Myarchive.zip:

```
wzzip -v Myarchive.zip
```

The next example adds all .log files in the c:\temp folder, except the log file named 072101.log, to a Zip file called Myarchive.zip:

```
wzzip -x072101.log Myarchive.zip c:\temp\*.log
```

This example adds files from a list in Mylist.txt, located in the c:\temp folder, to a Zip file called Myarchive.zip:

```
wzzip -a Myarchive.zip c:\temp\@Mylist.txt
```

The contents of Mylist.txt are shown here; they consist of six statements. The first statement begins with a semicolon (;), which makes it a comment that is ignored by WZZIP. The second and third lines specify two files in the current directory to be added to the archive. The fourth line identifies a file in the c:\MyFolder folder to be added to the archive. The fifth and sixth lines tell the WZZIP command to add all Microsoft Word and Excel documents in the current folder to the archive; each of these two lines ends with comments, which are ignored when the file is processed.

```
;This is a customized list of files to add to a new zip file
Mybook.pdf
MyFile.txt
C:\MyFolder\Myimage.jpg
*.doc ;Extract all Microsoft Word documents
*.xls ;Extract all Microsoft Excel Spreadsheets
```

Using the WZUNZIP.exe Command

Use the WZUNZIP command to unzip files and to perform an assortment of other related options, as demonstrated in the following examples. Detailed syntactical information on the WZUNZIP command is available in Appendix B, "WinZip Command-Line Support Add-on Reference."

The first example shows how to use the WZUNZIP command in its simplest form. In this case, the only argument passed to the WZUNZIP command is the name of the Zip file to extract. By default, all files in the archive are extracted to the current folder.

```
wzunzip Myarchive.zip
```

This example shows how to list all of the contents of the Myarchive.zip file:

```
wzunzip -v Myarchive.zip
```

This example extracts all .log files from the Myarchive.zip file:

```
wzunzip Myarchive.zip *.log
```

This example shows how to extract files from the Myarchive.zip file using the files listed in an external file named Mylist.txt:

```
wzunzip Myarchive.zip @Mylist.txt
```

Managing Your Archives with Scripts

As the previous examples have shown, using the WZZIP and WZUNZIP commands is a fairly straightforward process. However, since most people find it much easier to work from a GUI than from a command line, the previous examples are of limited advantage if you intend to use them only from the Windows command prompt or Run dialog box.

Given the number of options available with both of these commands, it's difficult to memorize them all. It would be much more helpful if you could type a list of one or more commands that you use often into a text file and then run them by simply double-clicking the text file, which is exactly what Windows shell scripts do.

In its most basic form, a Windows shell script is a text file containing one or more commands saved with a .bat file extension. Windows treats all files with this extension as executable files. When you double-click one, Windows opens it and executes each command that it finds in the file.

For example, using a simple text editor like Notepad, type the following commands and save the file with the name C:\Program Files\WinZip\Myscript.bat.

```
WZZIP C:\Myfolder\TextFiles.zip C:\Myfolder\*.txt
Pause
```

The first command listed is a WinZip command that creates a new archive in a folder named C:\MyFolder and adds all the .txt files located in the c:\Myfolder directory into it. If the TextFiles.zip archive already exists, the script updates its contents with all the .txt files found in the c:\Myfolders directory instead. The second statement in the file tells the script to pause until you press a key so that you can inspect the results of the command before the Windows command shell closes.

Next create a shortcut to the batch file on the Windows desktop and run it by double-clicking the shortcut icon. A Windows command session opens and processes your command, and the results are displayed along with a message telling you to press any key to continue, as shown in Figure 12-1.

Figure 12-1: Executing WinZip functionality from a Windows shell script

As you can see, you needed only two lines to create a simple script that you can run from your desktop to keep an archive updated by double-clicking it. You had to create the script only once, yet it can save you the trouble of starting WinZip and opening the archive and updating its contents every time you run it.

This example should give you some insight into the power of Windows shell scripting. To learn more about Windows shell scripting, have a look at my book entitled *Windows Shell Scripting and WSH Administrator's Guide*.[1]

---

[1] Ford Jr., Jerry Lee. *Microsoft Windows Shell Scripting and WSH Administrator's Guide.* Indianapolis, IN: Premier Press, 2001. ISBN: 1-931841-26-8.

A

KEYBOARD SHORTCUTS

WinZip provides a series of keyboard shortcuts that provide quick access to key product functionality. These shortcuts, summarized here, are visible on the WinZip Classic menus.

WHAT YOU'LL FIND

In this appendix, you will:

- Find a listing of WinZip keyboard shortcuts

Table A-1: WinZip Keyboard Shortcuts

Keystrokes	Description
F1	Activates WinZip help
F7	Activates the WinZip Move dialog box
F8	Activates the WinZip Copy dialog box
ALT + F4	Exits WinZip
CTRL + A	Selects all files in the currently open archive
CTRL + N	Activates the New Archive dialog box
CTRL + O	Activates the Open Archive dialog box
CTRL + P	Prints a file listing for the current archive
SHIFT + A	Activates the Add dialog box
SHIFT + C	Activates the CheckOut dialog box
SHIFT + D	Activates the Delete dialog box
SHIFT + E	Activates the Extract dialog box
SHIFT + F	Activates the Favorite Zip Folders dialog box
SHIFT + G	Activates the Comment dialog box
SHIFT + I	Installs desktop themes and screen savers
SHIFT + K	Activates WinZip Self-Extractor Personal Edition
SHIFT + L	Closes the archive
SHIFT + M	Opens an email screen and adds the archive as an attachment
SHIFT + R	Activates the Rename dialog box
SHIFT + S	Scans archives for viruses (if a virus scanner has been installed)
SHIFT + T	Checks the archive for errors
SHIFT + U	UUencodes the archive
SHIFT + V	Allows you to view the currently selected archive file
SHIFT + W	Switches WinZip between the Classic and Wizard modes

B

WINZIP COMMAND-LINE SUPPORT ADD-ON REFERENCE

The WinZip Command-Line Support Add-on is provided in the form of two commands: WZZIP and WZUNZIP. WZZIP is used to create and modify Zip files, and WZUNZIP is used to extract their contents. This appendix provides a detailed reference for both commands.

WZZIP

Use the WZZIP command to create new Zip files and to perform an assortment of other related options. Its command syntax is as follows:

```
wzzip [options] zipfilename [@listfile] [files]
```

The parameters shown within brackets are optional. When specifying parameters, separate each with a space. The parameters are as follows:

options. Tell WZUNZIP how you want to process the Zip file. If you do not specify any options, WZUNZIP automatically zips all files.

zipfilename. The name of the Zip file to create.

@listfile. A text file containing a list of the files to be added. Each file is listed on a separate line, and wildcard characters may be used.

files. A list of one or more files to be added to the Zip file.

The *options* parameter tells WZZIP what you want it to do. It may consist of a combination of any of the following arguments:

-a	Add file(s).
-a+	Remove the archive attribute from file(s) after zipping.
-b[*drive|path*]	Use the specified drive/path as the temporary location for files during an update operation.
-c	Add or modify Zip file comments.
-C	Add comments for files being added to a Zip file.
-d	Remove file(s) from a Zip file.
-e<x|n|f|s|0>	Specifies the compression level, as follows:

	-ex	Maximum compression
	-en	Normal compression
	-ef	Reduced compression
	-es	Minimal compression
	-e0	No compression

-f	Freshen files in the specified Zip file.
-h|-?	Display help.
-i[-]	Add file(s) that have their archive attribute set and then clears the archive attribute. To retain each file's archive attribute, use - (that is, -i-).
-jhrs	Do not add hidden, read-only, and system attributes.
-Jhrs	Add hidden, read-only, and system attributes. (This is the default.)
-k	Keep the Zip file's original date.
-m[f|u]	Move file(s) into the Zip file. You may, optionally, specify whether to freshen or update files in the archive.
-o	Change the Zip file's file date to match that of its newest file.
-p|P	Store all subfolder names.
-q	Show ANSI control codes inside comments.
-r	Recursively process subfolders. (Use this option in conjunction with -p or -P.)
-s[*password*]	Set a password.
-t[f][*date*]	Add file(s) newer or equal to the specified date. The default is the current date.
-T[f][*date*]	Add file(s) older than the specified date. The default is the current date.
-u	Update file(s) that have changed and add any new files.

-v[b|t][r][m][c]		View the files in the Zip file. Optional formats include the following:
[d|e|n|o|p|s][f]		
	b	Display brief information about the archive's contents, including file names, length, size, ratio, and date and time.
	t	Display technical information about the archive's contents, including file names, types, attributes, dates and times, compression methods, lengths, and the type of operating system that created the archive.
	r	Display archive contents in reverse sort order.
	m	Pause after each full screen.
	c	Show file comment if present.
	d	Sort by date.
	e	Sort by file extension.
	n	Sort by name.
	o	Sort in original order.
	p	Sort by percentage of compression.
	s	Sort by uncompressed size.
	f	Display date in *yyyy-mm-dd* format.
-vi[m]		View internal archive information. (Use m to keep text from scrolling off the screen.)
-whs		Add hidden and system files.
-Whs		Exclude hidden and system files.
-x<*filename*>		Exclude the specified file(s).
-x@*listfile*		Exclude any files listed in the specified listfile.
-yb[c]		Run in background mode. (Add c to automatically reply yes if prompted for a response.)
-yk		Convert file names to MS-DOS 8.3 character files names.
-yp		Add a "Press any key to continue" prompt to the end of the zip operation.
-z		Add or modify a comment.
-&[w]		Allow disk spanning. Use w to delete any files already on the disks.
[s[*drive*]]		Zip the entire specified drive.
-$[*drive*]		Store the volume label.
-@list		Simulate the creation of a Zip file and list the files that would be archived had this been a normal archive operation.
-^		Show the command line.

WZUNZIP

Use the WZUNZIP command to unzip files and to perform an assortment of other related operations. Its command syntax is as follows:

```
wzunzip [options] zipfilename [@listfile] [[drive:][\][path][\]] [files]
```

The parameters shown within brackets are optional. All parameters specified must be separated by a space.

options Tell WZUNZIP how to process the Zip file. If you do not specify any options, WZUNZIP automatically unzips all files.

zipfilename The name of the Zip file to unzip.

@listfile A text file containing a list of the files to be extracted. Each file is listed on a separate line, and you can use wildcard characters.

drive The drive where the Zip files reside.

path A path specifying the location of the Zip file.

files A list of one or more files to be extracted from the Zip file.

NOTE *If you do not specify either @listfile or specific files, WZUNZIP extracts all files in the archive.*

The *options* parameter tells WZUNZIP what you want it to do. It can consist of a combination of any of the following arguments:

-c[m]	Display file contents. (Use m to keep text from scrolling off the screen.)
-d	Re-create the folders for files stored in the Zip file. This option re-creates the original folder structure that the files were stored in on the computer where the archive was created.
-f	Refresh files in the target folder using matching files from the Zip file.
-h|-?	Show this help file.
-jhrs	Do not add hidden, read-only, and system attributes when unzipping.
-Jhrs	Apply hidden, read-only, and system attributes found in the Zip file. (This is the default.)
-n	Unzip file(s) and update any duplicates.
-o[-]	Overwrite duplicate files without prompting; use the optional - (that is, -o-) to reply no to prompts.
-p	Print a file.
-q	Show ANSI control codes inside comments.
-s[*password*]	Specify a password.
-t	Test the Zip file.

-v[b|t][r][m][c|	View the files in the Zip file. Optional formats include the following:	
d|e|n|o|p|s][f]		
	b	Brief.
	t	Technical.
	r	Reverse order.
	m	Pause after each full screen.
	c	Show file comment if present.
	d	Sort by date.
	e	Sort by file extension.
	n	Sort by name.
	o	Sort in original order.
	p	Sort by percentage of compression.
	s	Sort by uncompressed size.
	f	Display date in *yyyy-mm-dd* format.
-vi[m]	View internal archive information. (Use m to keep text from scrolling off the screen.)	
-x<*filename*>	Exclude the specified file(s).	
-x@*listfile*	Exclude any files listed in the specified listfile.	
-yb[c]	Run in background mode. (Add c to automatically reply yes if prompted for a response.)	
-yo	Replace hidden, system, and read-only files.	
-yp	Add a "Press any key to continue" prompt to the end of the zip operation.	
-ys	Replace spaces found in file names with the "_" character.	
-$	Restore the volume label on a floppy disk if specified in the Zip file.	
-@list	Simulate the extraction of a Zip file and list the files that would be unzipped had this been a normal archive operation.	
-^	Show the command line.	

WINZIP 8.1

WHAT YOU'LL FIND
In this appendix, you will:

- Review new WinZip features currently in the beta copy of WinZip

- Examine the WinZip beta's integration with Windows XP

Like most software programs, WinZip is a constantly evolving application. As of the writing of this book, the current version of WinZip is 8.0. However, the WinZip 8.1 beta version is also available. Software developers often prerelease beta versions of their applications to the general public to expose them to a wide test audience and to collect user feedback. Beta software is generally pretty sound, but there can be bugs, and users are warned up front of the risk of using beta software. Also, there is no guarantee that the features found in the beta program will actually end up in the final release version, or that new features won't suddenly appear, although generally the final product looks very much like its beta predecessor.

Sometimes applications undergo major revisions, and sometimes the changes are minor. Major product changes usually result in a new version number for the application. For example, an application might go from version 1.1 to version 2.0. When a version with minor changes is released, the first digit in its version number usually remains the same. For example, an application might go from version 2.0 to version 2.1. WinZip version 8.1 then does not represent a major product revision or upgrade. It does, however, provide some interesting enhancements to WinZip. This appendix will provide a review of the changes found in the beta version of WinZip 8.1.

As of the writing of this book, you can download a beta version of WinZip 8.1 and learn more about it from the WinZip website at www.winzip.com.

Introducing WinZip 8.1

WinZip 8.1 beta is an upgrade to WinZip 8.0. When the final version of WinZip 8.1 is released, it will be made available as a free download for currently registered WinZip users. WinZip 8.1 will run on any of the following operating systems:

- Windows 95
- Windows 98
- Windows ME
- Windows NT 4.0
- Windows 2000
- Windows XP

WinZip 8.1 installs using the same procedure that installs WinZip 8.0, as outlined in Chapter 2, "Installing and Managing WinZip." If you already have WinZip 8.0 installed, you can upgrade to the new version by closing any active WinZip windows and following the normal installation procedure.

Changes to the WinZip Wizard

The beta version of WinZip 8.1 offers enhanced capabilities for the WinZip Wizard. The wizard now allows you to run a setup or installation program if one is found inside a Zip file. In WinZip 8.0, you had to either unzip the archive using the WinZip Wizard and then run the setup or installation program, or use the WinZip Classic interface to run the programs.

The WinZip Wizard has also been enhanced to provide the ability to extract archives created using the WinZip disk spanning option. In WinZip 8.0, you could open spanned disk archives using only WinZip Classic.

New WinZip Classic Features

The beta version of WinZip 8.1 also includes enhancements to the WinZip Classic interface. For example, many of WinZip Classic's dialog boxes can now be resized to make them easier to work with. When extracting the contents of an archive, you can now select an option that tells WinZip to automatically open the folder where the archive's files have been extracted. With WinZip 8.0, you had to extract the files and then manually locate and open the target folder.

One significant enhancement to WinZip Classic is the addition of the Split feature. The Split feature allows you to arbitrarily split a larger archive into multiple files. When an archive is split, its first file will have a .z01 file extension, the second file will have a .z02 extension, and so on until the last file, which will have a .zip extension. The purpose of the Split feature is to help people who have email systems that limit the size of attachments. For example, if you use Yahoo's free email service, you are limited to an attachment with a maximum file size of 3MB. If you have a 5MB archive that you want to send to someone, you can use the WinZip Split feature to break the archive into two parts and then send each part as an attachment to separate emails. The recipient of your emails can then unzip the archive by opening the archive file with the .zip file extension.

To split an archive, it must be at least 64KB in size. After you create or open a Zip file, you can choose the Split option from the WinZip Classic Actions menu. The Split screen then appears as shown in Figure C-1.

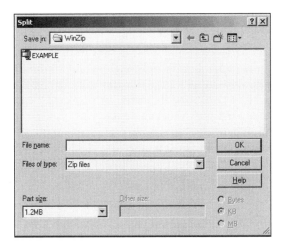

Figure C-1: The WinZip 8.1 Split feature lets you break large Zip files into smaller files

You must give the new split archive a different file name than the one assigned to the existing Zip file by typing the new name in the File name field. The Files of type field is used to filter the files displayed in the main display area. These are your options:

Zip files. Show only the Zip files in the currently selected folder.

All files. Show all files in the currently selected folder.

The Part size drop-down list lets you select the size of the files that will be created during the split operation. Your choices are these:

- 1.2
- 1.44
- 2.88
- 3
- 4
- 5
- Zip 100 Disk (100MB)
- CD-ROM (650MB)
- CD-ROM (700MB)
- Other size

If you choose the Other size option, then the Other size field is enabled, allowing you to type a file size of your own choosing. You do this by typing a number in the Other size field and then selecting the Bytes, KB, or MB option.

Other enhancements made to WinZip Classic include the ability to create Zip file comments of up to 64,000 characters. The Checkout feature has also been improved to allow you to check out up to 500 files. In WinZip 8.0, you were limited to a maximum of 50 files.

Tighter Windows Integration

Several new Windows integration improvements have been added to WinZip 8.1. For example, you can now select multiple Zip files from Windows Explorer and extract them in a single operation by right-clicking one of the files and selecting one of the WinZip extraction context menu options.

Another area where WinZip has improved its integration with Windows is the Zip and E-Mail Plus feature. It now includes a Password protect Zip file option, as shown in Figure C-2. When selected, this option lets you apply WinZip password protection to the archive file before it is automatically attached to your email.

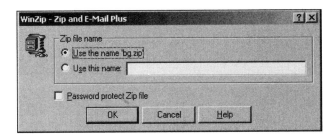

Figure C-2: The WinZip 8.1 Zip and E-Mail feature now includes an option to allow you to password protect your email attachment

Another Windows integration enhancement is the addition of a WinZip icon in the Windows System Tray. You can left-click the icon to start WinZip. Alternatively, you can right-click the WinZip icon and get single-click access to a number of WinZip features, as shown in Figure C-3, including these:

- Recently accessed Zip files
- Your WinZip Favorites folder
- A link to open WinZip
- WinZip's help system
- WinZip's About screen
- An option to temporarily or permanently remove the WinZip icon from the System Tray

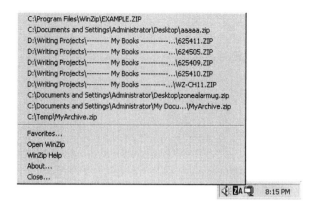

Figure C-3: WinZip 8.1 automatically adds a WinZip icon to the Window's System Tray to give you single-click access to WinZip

D

GLOSSARY

WHAT YOU'LL FIND
In this appendix, you will:

- Find a listing of terms and phrases used throughout this text

Add-on   A software application designed to interface with and extend the functionality of another software application.

ARC   An archive created by the ARC extraction utility that supports both compression and the grouping of more than one file into an archive.

ARJ   An archive created by an ARJ program that supports both compression and the grouping of more than one file into an archive.

Archive   A collection of files stored as a single file, usually in a compressed format.

Antivirus   A software program designed to detect malicious programs that attack computer systems and delete files, steal personal data, and cause an assortment of other problems.

Attribute   A quality of a Windows file or folder that governs a particular feature, such as the read-only attribute, which prevents a file or folder from being overridden, or the hidden attribute, which hides files from normal viewing.

Browser   A software program designed to operate over the Internet and present HTML content.

CAB   A type of archive known as a cabinet file used by Microsoft to group and compress files.

CheckOut   A WinZip feature that unzips archive contents to a temporary folder so that you can examine the files and then deletes the temporarily extracted files when you are done examining them.

Command Line   A text-based interface used to interact with Microsoft operating systems that also supports the development of scripts that can be used to automate common Windows processes.

Comments   Text associated with a Zip file that allows its creator to describe its contents or provide other useful information.

Compress   The act of reducing the amount of disk space required to store one or more files.

Decompress   The act of expanding a compressed file back into its original form.

Decryption   The process of decoding an encrypted file so that it can be viewed by Windows applications.

Disk Spanning   The process of storing a large Zip file over more than one removable store medium such as floppy disks.

Download   The process of retrieving a file from an Internet website and storing it on your computer for local processing.

Drag and Drop   The process of selecting one or more files and dropping them onto an application that is designed to process them, which in the case of WinZip, causes the application to open and display the file's contents.

Encryption   The process of encoding a file so that it cannot be viewed or read by another application unless it is first decoded.

Extract   The ability to unzip one or more files from an archive and copy them to a specified location.

FAQs   (Frequently Asked Questions) A collection of answers to questions that are commonly asked by users of software applications.

Favorite Zip Files   A feature of WinZip that allows you to manage all of your archives by identifying the folders that contain them.

File Extension   The component of a file name that appears after the last period (.), usually composed of three characters.

GZ   An archive typically found on Unix operating systems that supports the compression of a single file.

Keyboard Shortcut   A predefined combination of two or more keyboard keys that includes one modifier key (ctrl, shift, or alt) and at least one other key and is used to provide a shortcut to a specific application feature.

LZH An older type of archive that supports both the compression and grouping of one or more files in an archive.

Packed A value that indicates the size of the file as it exists inside an archive.

Password A secret code assigned to an archive that is required to decrypt and view the archive's contents.

Path The specification of the folder hierarchy that defines the location of a file on a computer.

Properties Attributes of a file that define its features and characteristics.

Ratio A measurement of the amount of compression that has been applied to a file inside an archive.

ReadMe.txt A Notepad file added to an archive that provides installation instructions or other useful information regarding the contents of an archive.

Registration Code A code provided by an application vendor upon payment for a copy of the vendor's software that removes the registration message and possibly enables additional functionality.

Screen Saver A software program that is designed to run on a computer when no user activity has occurred for a predefined period of time.

Self-Extracting Zip File A Zip file that includes a small program that allows the file to unzip itself when opened, without requiring the assistance of an external archive management program such as WinZip.

Shareware A method of distributing software that allows you to download a copy of the software from the Internet and use it for a specific period of time before deciding to purchase or uninstall it.

Shortcut A representation or link to a software program, file, or command that, when opened or activated, starts its associated application or executes its associated command.

TAR A type of archive file commonly used on Unix operating systems.

Theme A collection of desktop settings for wallpaper, colors, sounds, and so on that can be applied to the Windows desktop.

Toolbar A collection of icons that provides links to common application features usually located just under the application's menu bar.

Tool Tips An informational message that appears each time an application starts that is designed to provide the user with helpful hints and tips for using the application.

Unzip The act of extracting the contents of an archive.

UUencode The process of converting a binary file to a text file, which in the case of WinZip is designed to allow the transfer of binary files using older-style email systems.

Virus Scanner A software application designed to detect and remove harmful software programs that are deliberately designed to attack computer systems.

Wildcard   The use of the * and the ? characters to apply pattern matches to identify one or more files for a particular operation.

Winzip32.exe   The WinZip executable program.

WinZip Classic   A WinZip user interface designed for experienced users that provides access to all of WinZip's features and functionality.

WinZip Command-Line Support Add-on   An optional software program that provides additional support for executing WinZip functionality via a Windows command prompt or script.

WinZip Internet Browser Support Add-on   An optional software program that incorporates WinZip functionality into your Internet Explorer or Netscape Communicator Internet browser.

WinZip Self-Extractor   A WinZip application that allows you to create Zip files that can unzip their own contents when opened.

WinZip Tutor   A feature of the WinZip help system designed to step you through the basic use of WinZip and its most popular features.

WinZip Wizard   A specialized utility provided by WinZip that is designed to walk you step by step through the most common WinZip tasks, including the creation and extraction of Zip files.

Wzzip.exe   A WinZip command that allows you to create new Zip files from the Windows command prompt.

Wzunzip.exe   A WinZip command that allows you to unzip or extract the contents of Zip files from the Windows command prompt.

Z   An archive typically found on Unix operating systems that supports the compression of a single file.

Zip   An archive created by WinZip that enables the grouping of one or more compressed files.

Zip and E-Mail   A WinZip feature that can be used to automate the process of opening your email application and attaching a Zip file.

INDEX

.doc files, 83
DOS prompt, 106–107
downloads
    of archives from the Internet, 115–*116*
    location on hard drive of, 26
    of WinZip version 6.3, 13
    of WinZip version 8.1, 144
    of WinZip version 8.x, 7, 14
drag and drop. *See also* keyboard shortcuts; right-clicking the mouse
    adding files to archives, 34, 58, 101
    configuration options for, 80
    extracting files from archives, 61–*62*, 102
    printing files from archives, 103
    WinZip operations using, 99

E

email attachments
    file types supported by WinZip, 3
    mailing archives as, using drag and drop, 99
    mailing archives as, using Split feature, 144–145
    mailing archives as, with Classic interface, 55
    mailing archives as, with Wizard interface, 34
    password protection of, 146
encoded files, 3, 67–68
encryption, 46
.exe files
    automatic installation of, 72
    self-extracting, 126
Explorer. *See* Windows Explorer
external programs, setting up connections to, 81–*81*. *See also* add-ons for WinZip
Extract folder
    specifying default, in Classic interface, 77
    specifying default, in Wizard interface, 32, 36

extraction, 29
    with Classic interface, 59–61
    with Command-Line interface, 111
    WinZip 8.1's added capabilities, 146
    without opening WinZip, 101–102
    with Wizard interface, 31–*33*
Extract screen, 59, *60*, *61*, 102
    icons, *40*, *41*

F

FAQs, 92–*94*
Favorite Zip Folders
    adding and removing folders, 35
    icons, *40*, *41*
    naming subfolders, 26
    viewing, from Classic interface, 50
    viewing, from Wizard interface, *31*
    WinZip installation options for, 16, *17*
file attributes, 47
file compression. *See* compressed files; compression
file extensions
    .bat, 132
    .doc, 83
    encoded files, 3, 68
    .exe, 72, 126
    graphic files, 6
    setting up WinZip associations with, 17, 79, 83, 97
    .txt, 97
    .uue, 68
    WinZip-supported, *3*
    .zip, 3
filename argument, 109
files. *See also* archives (Zip files); context menus; files in archives
    paths to, 49
    system and hidden, 47, 109
    WinZip component, 96
files argument, 109–110

K

keyboard shortcuts. *See also* drag and drop; right-clicking the mouse
    adding multiple files to archives, 100
    Classic interface, 51–52, 135–136
    for configuring Classic interface toolbar, 77
    working with multiple archive files, 64

L

language options for self-extracting files, 125
.lha files, 2, *3*, 81
LHZ files, 2, *3*, 150
log of last action performed, 86

M

mail. *See* email attachments
Mail Archive option, 55
messages. *See also* comments
    configuring caution dialog box, 84
    creating, for self-extracting files, 123
Microsoft Windows. *See* Windows
Microsoft Word, opening archives in, 62
Miscellaneous property tab options, 74, 82–84, 104
Misc tab, 37, 38
Mouse configuration, 76
Move screen, 52–*53*
MS-DOS prompt, 106–107
multiple files in archives
    adding, 43, 46–47
    adding, keyboard shortcut for, 100
    deleting, 59, 60–61
    with duplicate names, 32, 58, 60–61
    viewing combined information about, 64–*65*

working with, 64–65
multitasking with WinZip, 83

N

Netscape Communicator, WinZip add-on for, 113
networking with WinZip, 6
    site licenses, 13
New Archive dialog box, 41, *42*
New Archive icons, *40, 41*

O

Open Archive screen, 48
    icons, *40, 41*
Open with WinZip screen, *63*
options arguments, 108–109, 111
Options dialog box in Wizard interface, 35–37
Options menu in Classic interface, *86. See also* Configuration options
    options on, 73–74
    Password option, 84–85
    Reuse WinZip Windows option, 85
    Save Settings options, 74, 86
    Set Installation Default option, 74, 86
    Sort option, 85
    View Last Output option, 86

P

packed value of an archive file, 151
Password argument, 109
Password button, 46
Password option, 73, 84–85
Password protect Zip file option, 146
Password screen, 46, *84*
paths to files and folders, 49
Program Locations property tab options, 74, 81–*82*

progress indicator screen, 84
properties of archives, 50–51

Q

quickview.exe (Windows program), 64

R

ratio, archive file, 151
readme files, advantages of comments over, 69
registration number, 21, 22
Reuse WinZip Windows option, 85
right-clicking the mouse. *See also* drag and drop; keyboard shortcuts
    adding files to archives, 100
    creating new archives, 30
    extracting archives, 101–102
    extracting multiple files in Windows Explorer, 146
    modifying archives, 58
    opening archives, 63
    previewing a file's contents, 64
    viewing Windows context windows, 95
    viewing WinZip menu options for files, 9
    working with archives, 9
Run dialog box, *106*
Run WinZip button, 67

S

Save full path info option, 49
screen savers
    configuring the installer, 83
    installing, with Classic interface, 72
    installing, with Wizard interface, 37
scripts, managing archives with, 132–133
Search button
    finding Zip folders with, 16
    options, 31

Select Activity box, 37
Select Buttons screen, 77
self-extracting files, 2
    creating, with Classic interface, 65–67
    creating, with WinZip Self-Extractor Add-on, 121–126
    with duplicate names, 125, 127
    running, 126–127
    specifying folder to extract to, 67, 123
    splash screen for, 123
    types of, 118
    WinZip Internet Browser Support Add-on and, 114
Self-Extractor Add-on, 117–127
    creating self-extracting files with, 121–126
    features, 118
    installing, 118–119
    making it the default option, 119
    registration screen, 120
    screen, 119–120
    uninstalling, 120
Self-Extractor Personal Edition screen, *66, 67*
shareware, 7
shortcuts. *See* desktop shortcuts; keyboard shortcuts
software
    installing with self-extracting files, 118, 127
    version numbers for, 143
Sort option, 73, 85
splash screen for self-extracting files, 123
Split feature, 144–146
starting WinZip
    with Command-Line interface, 107
    with WinZip 8.0 button, 18
    with Wizard interface, 26–27
Start menu, including WinZip on Windows', 17–18, 79
Start-up folder, specifying WinZip's, 77
startup interface, choosing, 37, 38
Start-up options for WinZip, 82
Switch Interface dialog box, 37–38

system files, 47, 109
System property tab options, 74, 78–80, 103–*104*

T

TAR files, 2, *3*, 83
technical support, 23. *See also* Help
Temp folder, 78
Test option, 68–69, 126
   for self-extracting files, 126
themes. *See* desktop themes
Tip of the Day option, 18–*19*
   turning on and off, 60
toolbars
   Classic interface, 40–41
   Classic interface, Toolbar
     property tab options, 74, 76–77
   Help Topics screen, 28, 90
   Windows Explorer, Classic
     interface imitation of, *41*, 83
tool tips, 76
Tutorials for WinZip, 90–*91*

U

unzipping. *See* extraction
Use shell extension option, 103, *104*
UUencode option, 67–68

V

View button, 83
viewer applications
   configuring, 81
   displaying list of, 83
   to use with WinZip, 64
View Last Output screen, 68–69, 74, 86, *86*
View property tab options, 74–76
View screen, 63, *64*
   icons, *40, 41*
Virus scan option, 65, 71

W

warning messages, configuring, 84
wildcard characters, 43, 46–47
Windows 3.1
   naming archives for computers
     with, 46
   WinZip version to use with, 13
Windows 95 and later versions
   command prompt, 106–107
   file-viewing applications, 64
   integration with WinZip 8.1 beta
     version, 146
   integration with WinZip 8.x,
     8–9, 80, 95–104
Windows applications, opening
   archives in, 62
Windows command line. *See*
   Command-Line interface
Windows Explorer
   configuring, for use of WinZip
     with, 80
   displaying extracted files in, 32, *33*
   extracting multiple files in, 146
   toolbar, Classic interface
     imitation of, *41*, 83
Windows Run dialog box, 105, 106
Windows shell scripts, 132
Windows Start menu, including
   WinZip in, 17–18, 79
Windows System Tray, putting
   WinZip icon in, 146, *147*
WinZip 8.0 button, 18
WinZip 8.x. *See also* add-ons for
   WinZip
   advanced capabilities, 6
   configuring, with Classic
     interface, 44–47, 73–86
   configuring, with Wizard
     interface, 35–37
   default location on hard drive,
     20
   disk spanning limitations, 45
   how to download, 7, 14
   installing, 14–18
   integration with Windows, 8–9,
     80, 95–104
   license agreement, 21, *22*

STEAL THIS COMPUTER BOOK 2
What They Won't Tell You About the Internet

by WALLACE WANG

In the same informative, irreverent, and entertaining style that made the first edition a bestseller, this edition covers Internet security issues like viruses, cracking, and password theft. The CD-ROM contains over 200 anti-hacker and security tools for Windows, Macintosh, and Linux.

2000, 400 PP. W/CD-ROM, $24.95 ($37.95 CDN)
ISBN 1-886411-42-5

THE OPERA 5.X BOOK
Browsing the Web with Speed and Style

by J.S. LYSTER

The Opera web browser is fast, compact, configurable, and standards-compliant. Learn to take full advantage of Opera's powerful features, including how to open multiple windows, retrieve multiple documents simultaneously, and navigate entirely with the keyboard. The CD-ROM includes trial versions of Opera 5.x for all platforms, as well as other utilities and plug-ins.

2001, 336 PP. W/CD-ROM, $29.95 ($44.95 CDN)
ISBN 1-886411-47-6

JOE NAGATA'S LEGO® MINDSTORMS™ IDEA BOOK

by JOE NAGATA

The LEGO MINDSTORMS Robotics Invention System from LEGO combines LEGO bricks with a programmable brain, making it easy to create working robots. This book shows readers how to build 10 exciting robots using LEGO MINDSTORMS, with over 250 step-by-step illustrations.

2001, 184 PP., $21.95 ($32.95 CDN)
ISBN 1-886411-40-9

THE BOOK OF JAVASCRIPT

A Practical Guide to Interactive Web Pages

by THAU!

Rather than offer cut-and-paste solutions, this tutorial/reference focuses on understanding JavaScript, and shows web designers how to customize and implement JavaScript on their sites. The CD-ROM includes code for each example in the book, script libraries, and relevant software.

2000, 424 PP. W/CD-ROM, $29.95 ($44.95 CDN)
ISBN 1-886411-36-0

THE LINUX COOKBOOK

Tips and Techniques for Everyday Use

by MICHAEL STUTZ

Over 1,500 step-by-step "recipes" show how to use Linux for everyday tasks, including printing; converting and managing files; editing and formatting text; working with digital audio; creating and manipulating graphics; and connect to the Internet.

2001, 396 PP., $29.95 ($44.95 CDN)
ISBN 1-886411-48-4

Phone:

1 (800) 420-7240 OR
(415) 863-9900
MONDAY THROUGH FRIDAY,
9 A.M. TO 5 P.M. (PST)

Fax:

(415) 863-9950
24 HOURS A DAY,
7 DAYS A WEEK

Email:

SALES@NOSTARCH.COM

Web:

HTTP://WWW.NOSTARCH.COM

Mail:

NO STARCH PRESS
555 DE HARO STREET, SUITE 250
SAN FRANCISCO, CA 94107
USA

Distributed in the U.S. by Publishers Group West

UPDATES

This book was carefully reviewed for technical accuracy, but it's inevitable that some things will change after the book goes to press. Visit **http://www.nostarch.com/ winzip_updates.htm** for updates, errata, and other information.